OUR MAKER LIFE

OUR MAKER LIFE

KNIT AND CROCHET PATTERNS, INSPIRATION, AND TALES FROM THE CREATIVE COMMUNITY

ABRAMS, NEW YORK

CONTENTS

INTRODUCTION: WHO IS OML?

We live in a world that is constantly changing. Constantly moving. Constantly evolving. And constantly growing. We aim to stop and make in a world that requires us to simultaneously keep moving while learning to slow down. At times, the world forces us to release the control of that flow and become a bit more still, a bit quieter, a bit more focused on turning the page to what truly matters. We have always been focused on this beautiful combination of growth, slow living, and surrendering to the flow. We realize how inherent it is for our team, our makers, our creative industry, and ultimately for the advancement and evolution of our world—a world that in so many ways is this beautiful melodic symphony, and we are the composers.

As our world moves and shifts, ebbs and flows, we strive to remain concrete: Our Maker Life (OML) is a movement for makers by makers, and was launched in May 2016. The OML community consists of knitters, crocheters, yarn dyers, business owners, pattern designers, bloggers, social media influencers, and other fiber artists who are passionate about contributing creatively and collectively to the handmade. What began as an idea by five makers to hop offline and meet up in person has grown into a community of more than 115,000 fellow makers passionate about the fiber arts. Our vision and mission? To come and join together for networking, connection, inspiration, and making. The OML dream team loves the maker life and—as knitters, crocheters, and yarn dyers ourselves—works hard to connect creatives and industry professionals, to feature the best in handmade, and to organize annual international maker meetup events.

Our philosophy has remained concrete as well: Hold tight to passion, always create with integrity, make with diversity in mind, and never stop accomplishing—this is the core of our maker movement. OML is continuously moving forward, innovating, and improving. Before, during, and after we work with our yarn, goodness is always near: We aim to always be honest, transparent, and fair. Our community trusts us and knows they can take us at our word, and that we support, collaborate, and stand for those who make with an equally honest and ethically valuable contribution. Our team has and will always remain diverse: We know that our community is composed of people with different ideas, strengths, interests, dreams, and cultural backgrounds, and that those attributes are what make the OML family profoundly great. We strive to work our hardest and are determined to amplify both the majority and minority voice. We aim to be leaders in creating a safe space, encouraging healthy debate and differences of opinion both on our online platforms and at our offline events.

And finally, we are always working. Creativity and fiber art are the foundation of what we do, showcasing and highlighting knit and crochet excellence as a core value. We focus on fun and celebration through modern style and technology. We move with courage, boldness, and care for others. We are open to change, growth, and at times being uncomfortable— because we know that we stand to lose so much without it. We build social value with the maker in mind and hold no place for those who seek to gain with selfish motives, or in ways that make others feel unsupported and undervalued. We hold zero tolerance for not crediting creative work as original art, as the use of dynamic fiber, pattern, and design drives our organization. These values outline and are an underlying note to our core philosophies.

Jewell, OML founder, currently serves on the OML leadership team for event organization, marketing, editorial publication, and business development. She hosts the OML podcasts, loves to blog, and is the owner of Northknits Handmade Knitwear. She also has an extensive chunky yarn stash that she is quite proud of.

Nathan, OML co-founder, currently serves on the OML leadership team for event organization, merchandise sales, graphics, and technical advancement. He loves knitting, pattern designing, and photography on an expert level, and is the owner of Loopn' Threads. He also has a heart for cabling cowls and all things chocolate.

Jake currently serves on the OML leadership team for event organization, brand correspondence, marketing, and social media. He loves to keep a clean inbox, dye yarn, knit, and crochet, and is the owner of Kenyarn Hand Dyed Yarn. He also has the team beat on daily steps and exercise miles run.

Christie currently serves on the OML leadership team for event organization, brand correspondence,

social media, and content development. She loves dry humor, knitting sweaters, and pattern designing, and is the owner of Christie Bodden Designs. She also works at Beehive Wool Shop, a rad and historic knitting store in Victoria, BC.

Alison, Kelly, and Kathleen, retired OML founders, are three integral and irreplaceable makers who supported and encouraged OML's jump start and subsequent growth from day one to year three.

At our core, we are a team of creative and diverse individuals who desire to reach an entire global community, woven and connected by a deep love for yarn. We make, we laugh, we showcase, and we dance—to the best literal and philosophical good tunes. Ludwig van Beethoven once said that it seemed unthinkable to leave the world before he had produced all that he felt called upon to produce. We like to think Beethoven was onto something, as our organization holds a similar sentiment. We desire to spend our time producing within our calling, and we know that we have discovered a unique, beautiful melody that helps our world, community, and each one of us as creatives sing through yarn. Beethoven made melodies, and they were among the world's most beautiful ones. This book is an ambitious, passionate, and printed effort to do just that: make the best yarnish melodies.

We hope that in our ever-changing world, you get a sense of who we are, and that through your own change, movement, evolvement, and growth, we inspire you to make.

xx, OML

ABOUT THIS BOOK

Books have been a part of our daily lives since ancient times. They have been used for telling stories, archiving history, and sharing information about our world. And it has always felt natural to our team to share OML in book form. So, what is this book all about and what will you find in these pages? Two things: maker stories and patterns. We've collected knit and crochet patterns, maker highlights, and inspiring tales to share with you, and we're incredibly humbled and proud to be able to do so.

First up is **Part One: Maker Stories**. This book includes great stories centered around knit, crochet, weaving, and yarn dyeing. The written word is a powerful storytelling tool, and the aim of this section is to authentically share the creative maker journey. These stories are voiced with humor, heartfulness, and candidness. They give insight to both past and present memories. These stories push beyond the typical blog post or shop bio and instead offer the opportunity to delve a little deeper and get to know a maker in a way that feels like meeting up at a coffee shop to chat.

Every maker has a story—dreams, goals, and triumphs—and our aim is to uplift and highlight the very essence of each. Stories like that of Kristine Rodriguez, who tells of her path not yet seen. She is the knitter and founder of Declarative, a sustainable knitwear brand designed to serve women throughout all seasons of the year. Using spools of yarn and her hand-powered knitting machine, Kristine handcrafts each garment out of her Seattle, Washington, studio. *During a typical day in the studio, I'm jumping between my sketchbook, computer, and knitting machine*, Kristine writes. We hope that you will be able to relate to Kristine and the rest of her words and the images alongside them, as both create a dynamic story through and through.

Stories like Jennifer Sylvester's, who tells of her journey to dyeing. Jen is the indie dyer and slow knitter behind Laine and Lotus Fiber Co., a New England–based shop featuring small-batch, hand-dyed yarn. Her love of fiber arts is ever expanding, and she truly feels she was meant to express her creative soul through her yarn. *Like many other makers, my introduction to the fiber world came at a time when I was feeling lost*, Jen writes. In profoundly vast and different ways, many of us have felt lost as makers. We hope that you will be able to relate to her and remember that, yes, we can lose ourselves on the craft journey, but we can find ourselves too—and experiencing and realizing both ultimately brings the adventure full circle.

OML believes a maker pic is worth a thousand words, and our visual stories highlight that belief to the fullest. Stories like that of Montana Crochet. She shows her place—a beautiful, cozy two-room cabin hidden in the Helena-Lewis and Clark National Forest outside of Helena, Montana. *This is our sanctuary.*

Even in the winter, when snowdrifts the size of single-story buildings cover our access road, we jump on our snowmobiles and trek up the mountain, two kids and our dog in tow, to soak up the mountain air and, most importantly, the silence. Many of us know that silence and often crave it while we make.

Stories like that of Jake of Kenyarn, who brings his talent and passion to the OML leadership team while equally completely rocking it as a yarn dyer. *Dyeing yarn is about finding the magic in the world and bringing it to life with color. It is about turning emotion into color. Holding a colorway is more than just how it feels in your hands; it's about how it makes you feel in your heart.* When friends ask Jake how he comes up with colorways, he tells them it's simple—find what you love and make it your palette. Whether you dye yarn or not, we hope you get a true sense of the love and passion he describes and shows.

And then **Part Two: The Patterns**. Oh yes, the *patterns*. On our social platforms, at our events, and even on our merch, we have said it before and we'll keep saying it: All we do is make, make, make. Our pattern section showcases some of the best DIY knit/crochet vibes out there, all exclusively here for you, our readers, to enjoy, including a headband, some hats, a cowl, sweaters, socks, a dress, and more. We hope you find patterns to help hone your skills, to challenge yourself with, to inspire, and to make your own.

So, **what will you find?** From the first page to the last, our community and industry has amazing, compelling stories, and this book shows makers well beyond the standard online bio or Q&A interview. If these individuals could sit down with you over coffee, these are the stories they would share about their handmade journey: what makes them unique, how they got started in their craft, the passion that drives their business. In this book, you will find the vision, inspiration, funny story, motto, faith, etc. behind *their maker life*. These stories are truly written from the heart, with original content that showcases maker style, diversity, and personality. You will find journeys into the creative lives of the maker photographer, reflecting who they are as a handmade artisan, fashion designer, style influencer, craft enthusiast, indie dyer, and more. You will find what we love to highlight—the beauty of handmade with the knit/crochet designer themselves or someone else modeling their knitwear, a look at their workspace, what inspires their work, and/or what makes their everyday life in the fiber arts world beautiful. Our community has myriad amazing, creative, and talented pattern designers, and this book aims to showcase some of them. We love our patterns and know there is nothing better than settling in and getting your DIY on—and you will find great designs that we are proud to present.

Knitting is the process of using two or more needles to loop yarn into a series of interconnected loops to create a finished garment or some other type of fabric. Crochet is a process of creating textiles by using a crochet hook to interlock loops of yarn, thread, or strands of other materials. Yarn dyeing is the dyeing of the yarns before they have been made into fabrics. Through stories, visual lifestyle, and patterns you will finish this book loving the creative fiber arts process and opening the book again and again to embrace and enjoy every page. And we hope that by the end you'll be fully immersed in *our maker life*.

PART ONE

maker stories

WHAT IT MEANS TO BE A MAKER

Maker: noun; defined as a person or thing that makes. Maker is also defined as a manufacturer, a poet, sometimes even given the attribute of a Higher Power. And for makers in the craft of fiber arts, many would no doubt adhere to a sense of calm spirituality when yarn, needle, and hook are in motion. But *what does it mean to be a maker*, really? It is one question that, over the years, OML has discovered breeds a multitude of answers. For some, making is peace and release from anxiety, hurt, and pain. For others, it is business, hustle, and career. For some of us, it comprises those sweet moments spent with family and friends. For others still, it is the essence of coolness, creativity, and joy. For many, it is a combination of all these things. And for some, it really is just being a person that makes—where we can take a moment to pause the spiraling movement of the world, while simultaneously just having something to do with our hands. One thing that OML has found to be a constant in what it means to be a maker is *community*.

In starting our movement, we believed it important to create and promote community, both virtually and offline. Why? The same technology that keeps us connected more easily than ever also creates a risk of interference with the opportunity to develop meaningful, personal relationships, and we saw a powerful and immersive opportunity for the likes of online

and IRL to be woven together through the beauty of yarn. We knew that there was strong value in sharing our collective work and passion for the fiber arts. We trusted that there was worth in meeting in person at our city events to inspire and educate. We felt deep down that there was a need for a space to share our brands, businesses, and stories in both blog and conference. Most importantly, we realized that community sat at the core of all that we knew, trusted, and felt, and we believe it still.

For us, community is indeed the cast-on to why so many of us make. Some may say that *community* is a noun simply describing a collective of people. But so many more of us would agree that community can also be a sort of verb—a near active, living thing that has motion and impact. That energy has created a movement more than 115,000 OML makers strong. Creative and diverse souls developing and transferring an intelligent, supportive, powerful, and immersive energy the world through, and defined by so many of us, simply, as *love*. In the years since our first social media post, in-person conference, and stories shared in print, we have discovered that OML is very much personified as *togetherness* (and we know that cozy yarn brings people together in a beautiful and profound way). Community and love define what it means to be a maker for our team, and we know it is the same definition for many of you. It is the start and continuation of our story, and of so many of yours.

Community. Love. Sharing stories. The culmination of such sparks an energetic light that acts as a heartbeat to the very definition of Our Maker Life, both written and visual. In actuality, we could long debate about what it *means* to be a maker, but the beauty of it all is that our stories really drive that conversation. Our stories *create* that conversation. Our stories give *feeling* to that conversation. Part One serves as a place to tell it all, and we feel both honored and privileged to share these words. Here, you will read about makers' peace and release from anxiety, hurt, and pain. You will read about the business, hustle, and career; the moments spent with family and friends. You will read about how knitting and crochet and weaving and yarn dyeing are cool, creative, and spark joy. You will read about how in a moment, the entire world can spiral in a way we never thought it quite would and yet we can pause, pick up our yarn, take a breath, and have something beautiful to do with our hands.

I found Our Maker Life when I truly needed it the most. I felt like a solo act, desperate for meaningful connection and relationships with people who understand the creative process and its vulnerability. Diving headfirst into the OML community has been transformative. This organization is more than just a summer meetup. It is a community, a family, and a mentality.

—Jake, OML team

In reality, anyone who creates things can be a maker. The term itself is an identity to what you conjure up. The bigger picture is the maker movement itself, because no matter what you make, together we push the community forward. Every niche may not be the forefront but there is strength in numbers.

—Nathan, OML team

To me, OML is all about unconditional love and support. Makers for makers, no matter who you are, and a community open to every single human. Making brings us together, unites us, and the love—that true, authentic, genuine love—in the best and purest way binds us together.

—Christie, OML team

I am learning to accept who I am through and through, to believe in myself, to trust those who support me and who believe in the OML brand and vision—past, present, and future. I am proud of myself and what that looks like from a maker perspective, and I subsequently challenge our community to celebrate diversity from color of skin to color of skein, because that and everything in between is what makes us makers. These are founding cores for everything we do and create, and that won't ever change.

—Jewell, OML team

This book is our community. This book is our love. These are our maker stories.

THE PATH NOT YET SEEN

Bio : Kristine Rodriguez is the knitter and founder of Declarative, a sustainable knitwear brand designed to serve women throughout the seasons of the year, for many years to come. Using spools of yarn and her hand-powered knitting machine, Kristine handcrafts each garment out of her Seattle, Washington, studio.

Visit declarativethelabel.com or follow @declarativethelabel to see what she's currently working on.

Photography: Marcella Ratsamy, @marcellarphoto

During a typical day in the studio, I'm jumping between my sketchbook, computer, and knitting machine, diligently working, obsessing over details, and listening to true-crime podcasts in the background. Among my samples and yarn, you'd probably think that I am very much in my element as a knitter, business owner, and "all-hats" person behind Declarative. However, I must confess that I never intended to be any of these things. I was just someone who studied the wrong thing in college, as many people do.

I majored in graphic design. Honestly, I could've told you after the first week that it wasn't the right fit for me. While my friends were excited to finally start their majors, I was jealous of the textiles students, who were stapling fabric into their swatch books. Don't get me wrong, there were aspects of graphic design that I enjoyed. But I didn't like working on a computer all day (which is pretty problematic, given the nature of graphic design). Without another direction in mind, I stuck with it. It wasn't until my last semester that I discovered the knitting machine in an elective class. This turned out to be the change I was looking for.

I'm not exaggerating when I say that it was love at first knit. My whole semester became dedicated to the knitting machine. I spent countless hours in the studio testing out ideas and experimenting with different yarns. Unlike my graphic design projects, knitting felt more like play rather than work. It felt right.

Since it was a little too late in the game to change my major, I graduated with this one class under my belt and knitwear as my new direction.

After finishing school, I applied for a bunch of knitwear positions. It took a while, but I finally landed an internship that eventually snowballed into a dream job, and the rest is history . . . just kidding!

What actually happened? You might already know the answer—I entered the workforce completely unqualified to pursue this new passion. Somewhere out there is a stack of unanswered job applications as proof. At the time, the rejection was defeating. I couldn't help feeling like a massive failure. That I'd found knitting too late and missed my chance to have the career I wanted. But what I used to view as failure turned out to be a gift. Unable to get a knitwear job, I eventually chose to create one for myself.

Naturally, this happened over brunch. (Where else do good ideas happen?) I can't tell you why that morning was different. Maybe my chai latte was spicier than usual. Maybe a magical hawk flew overhead. Whatever the reason, that morning was different. *I* was different. After two years of working dead-end graphic design and retail gigs, I decided to go for it. Sitting in front of my brunch, I committed myself to starting a knitwear line. I had no clue how I would do it (note: I hardly knew how to knit at the time), but I got to work, one garment at a time.

Back then the imposter syndrome was real. I was a graphic designer trying to be a knitter, literally ask-

ing the basics like, "How do I make clothes? What's my aesthetic? They say you're supposed to slope the shoulder, but do you really need to?" (The answer is often yes, by the way.) Looking back at those early collections, I must first apologize for all of the crop tops. Secondly, I think what I created was more of what I thought handmade knitwear was supposed to be rather than what was true to me.

Slowly but surely, I found my way. Five years, eight collections, and many missteps later, I'm no longer a graphic designer trying to be a knitter. I'm just a knitter, whose graphic design background has shaped my creative voice and continues to inspire my most fulfilling projects. It's pretty ironic, really.

I beat myself up for so long over "wasting" my college years studying the wrong thing, but I couldn't be more thankful for it now. I've come to appreciate what graphic design allows me to bring to the table as a knitter. Skills like layout, typography, and visual communication empower me to make clothes that are functional as well as conceptual. Sometimes they're even meaningful. That part of the process is why I love knitting the most.

A perfect example is the first type-based knit I ever made, the "Wake Up and Dream" sweater. This intarsia piece is a strong overlap between knitting and graphic design, and creating it was one of the most fulfilling experiences I've had as a maker. Unlike my usual design process, this project just flowed out of me (that sounds gross, but you know what I mean). The project was challenging, and the process of figuring it out felt engaging and energetic—sketching thumbnails, picking fonts, laying everything out on the computer and translating it into a pattern by hand. I rotated between my sketchbook, computer, and knitting machine until I'd finally crafted a knit that was both legible and visually expressive, just as any graphic designer does. Without a doubt, this project breathed life back into me as a knitter. More than that, it felt like me.

It's amazing how things happen like that. The journey feels so chaotic and fruitless in the moment. Then you turn around one day and see that it was a clear path all along. A random elective class can be the change you were seeking. The struggle to find a job can blossom into a business. Years spent studying the wrong major can come back into the fold and inspire some of your best work. Regardless of how it might seem in the moment, time is never wasted.

MONTANA CROCHET

Bio : Ashley Schneider is the dyer, designer, and one-woman show behind Montana Crochet, based out of Great Falls and Bald Butte City, Montana. As a proud third-generation Montanan, she loves exploring and discovering new hidden gems that the state has to offer, and spends as much time at her cabin hidden in the mountains as possible.

You can find Ashley at @montana.crochet and on her website at montanacrochet.com.

*T*his place of ours—our little two-room cabin hidden in the Helena-Lewis and Clark National Forest outside of Helena, Montana—this is our sanctuary. Even in the winter, when snowdrifts the size of single-story buildings cover our access road, we jump on our snowmobiles and trek up the mountain, two kids and our dog in tow, to soak up the mountain air and, most importantly, the silence.

You see, there's a certain silence you experience deep in the mountains away from electricity, running water, and people. You can hear the wind rolling through the trees before you begin to feel it. Sometimes it's so still, you can hear the sound that a snowflake makes when it settles on the front porch.

This cabin and the surrounding area is the place that I draw my dyeing inspiration from. Whether it's the first Indian paintbrush that pokes through the ground in the spring, an abandoned gold mine tucked up and hidden in a hillside, or the color of lichen growing for decades on granite boulders . . . inspiration is everywhere.

A few years back, my man showed up at the cabin after a solo ride on the snowmobile. Covered in snow and with his glasses completely fogged up, he busted through the door:

"I need your camera."

"What? Like, my big-girl camera?"

"Yes, *right now*."

I tossed him my camera bag and watched him rush up the hillside with a tail of snow flying in his wake, and then he suddenly stopped and turned back around to face our cabin. The image that he took that early evening in January 2016 is the image I used as my inspiration for this project. The colors in that moment were ethereal. They were stunning. And it's that image that reminds me of how magical this place is.

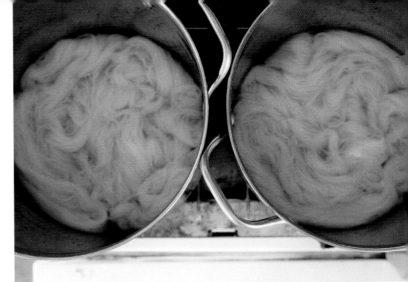

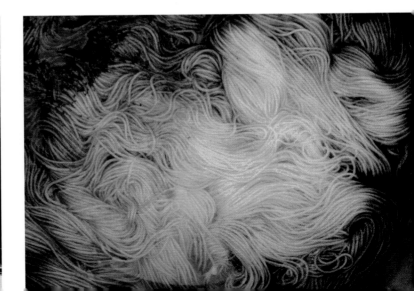

HELLO LAVENDER

Bio **:** Reshma is the owner and maker behind Hello Lavender. She's a knitter, crocheter, indie yarn dyer, and polymer clay artist. You can spot her draped in mustard yellow and running off a steady intake of coffee (and/or wine) to bring you handcrafted stitch markers, modern jewelry, and hand-dyed yarn.

Find more of her at hellolavender.com.

Photography: Sonya Kammes Photography, sonyakammes.com

*L*ighter skin is more beautiful; doctor and engineer are the best careers; long hair is prettier; men always eat first; women must know how to take care of a house; no dating; marry within your culture; you're getting fat and need to lose weight. Those statements, and countless more just like them, filled my childhood and spilled over into my adolescence. I didn't just hear them from my parents, but from relatives, other Indians, Bollywood, and Indian TV. These morals were ingrained into my brain to such a point that they impacted how I planned my life as I got older. I felt insecure, as I had darker skin. I thought I was fat, which led to horrible body image issues. I was afraid to cut my hair because I wanted to be beautiful. I was terrified to talk to boys, let alone be friends with any. I loved the arts but told myself I could never pursue a career in them.

At this point I should probably tell you that I do, in fact, love my parents immensely. The things they told me when I was growing up were just a reflection of how they grew up and what they knew. They're part of the Indian culture, generations and generations of Indians thinking this way and passing it down to their kids. Even though I respect my parents and my culture, I wanted to see some change. I wanted to be seen as equal to men. I wanted to get a degree in something I cared about. I wanted to date. I wanted to be myself and not get judged for it. I wanted to cut my hair and still feel beautiful. I didn't want to fear getting a few shades darker in the summer. I wanted

to do so much but didn't know how, because I feared I would be a disappointment. It wasn't until my late teens and early twenties that I started to challenge what I had been told my entire life. With pushing these boundaries came a lot of struggle, disagreements, disappointment, fear, and sadness for both my parents and me.

I started dating the whitest boy imaginable in high school. No, really, the whitest. Nope, whiter than that. Whiter still. I didn't date him to shove it in anyone's face, or as some rebellious challenge to authority, but because I truly loved this boy, and SPOILER ALERT: I married him! Even though my first major in college was psychology, I switched after a year to fine arts. I cut my hair. Now, these may seem like small things to most people, but for me they were huge. The constant fear of rejection and disapproval from my parents was always on my mind. I think it's safe to say we all seek approval from our parents, right?

I've always struggled with confidence and knowing who I am as a person, probably because for the longest time I was suppressing all those feelings. Even when I was working a nine-to-five job as a graphic designer, I wasn't happy or fulfilled. Sure, I had an artistic job, but even then something was missing. It wasn't until after I had my first daughter and quit my job that it dawned on me that I needed to be my own boss, make my own art, and open my own business. I'd learned to crochet from my mom when I was ten years old. I fell in love with the craft and with yarn

because of her, but it was never supposed to be a career. It was instead relegated to the area of our lives where dreams go to die: a hobby.

When relatives or other Indians ask me what I do, I explain it and get the same looks and varying forms of the same question: "How are you going to make money?" "But isn't that a hobby? How do you make a living?" Granted, I'm not making the big bucks like a doctor or engineer (yet!), but isn't happiness worth more than making a lot of money? I contribute to my family. My business helps pay the bills. This job allows me to be home with my kids, which is immensely more valuable to me than adding another zero to our tax return.

I'm usually viewed as a "bad" Indian in so many ways. I married out of my culture, I don't have a traditional job, and a truckload of other stuff that, if listed, would have the word count of this essay bursting at the seams. I respect my culture, I truly do. I just think there are aspects of it that are heavily outdated. Who I married has nothing to do with being an Indian. The length of my hair and the level of darkness of my skin have nothing to do with being an Indian. Fighting against values like these should not be the norm, but it is for so many fellow Indians. Hopefully with new generations these outdated ideas will start to fade, and instead values such as diversity, independence, creativity, and individuality will be held as the new standard and celebrated instead of feared.

I am very proud to be an Indian woman. My work is heavily influenced by my culture and upbringing. The colors I choose to work with are a representation of my culture—bold, vibrant, and full of meaning. It only took me a hair over thirty years to find myself, but I finally feel I'm in a place where I can be myself and not feel ashamed. I have met so many amazing, strong, independent women in my journey to start my own business and am surrounded by confident and supportive women who encourage one another. I'm able to use my creativity like I've always wanted to. I still get the feeling from time to time that my parents don't fully understand what I do for a living, and that's fine. But I do know they are proud of me. As much as I've grown through this journey, so have they. For what feels like the first time in my life, I'm clear on who I am, and in that clarity, I know that my parents will be fine, and so will I.

My strength defines who I am as an Indian. My creativity defines who I am as an Indian. My ambition defines who I am as an Indian.

I define who I am as an Indian.

THE FYNBOS KINGDOM

Bio : Madeleine Botha worked as a graphic designer for more than a decade before stumbling into indie yarn dyeing in 2017. She creates color palettes that speak of her daily observations and inspirations.

Follow her on Instagram @yama_fibre_art and visit her online store at www.yamayarn.com.

Photography by Madeleine Botha and Reto Mani

*B*rown-looking, scratchy vegetation clothes the mountains and lowlands of the Western and Eastern Cape provinces of South Africa. This unique kind of shrubland, or heathland vegetation, makes up 80 percent of the Cape Floral Kingdom and is called "fynbos," derived from the Dutch word *Fijnboch*, which means "fine bush." The species diversity of fynbos is one of the main things that makes it so special: Table Mountain alone has more species of plants than the whole of the British Isles. The fynbos biome is home to one of the world's richest floras, with more than nine thousand species of plants occurring within an area the size of Malawi or Portugal. Two-thirds of these species are endemic to the region, meaning that they occur nowhere else on earth. In addition, when looking at diversity at the macroscale within fynbos vegetation, it is home to between 150 and 170 unique species per 1,000 kilometers, thus making it two to three times more species diverse than the world's rain forests.

Here, in a laid-back coastal suburb called Noordhoek, is where I call home and where you'll find my business—Yama Hand Dyed Yarn. The word "Yama" is layered with meaning from different mythologies and languages, some rather dark, but in Japanese it means "mountain." I draw inspiration from the natural beauty around me, from my own indigenous garden, the wonderful Kirstenbosch National Botanical Garden, and the greater Western Cape landscape, including the West Coast and the Klein Karoo. It's an incredible place to create and a place that enables me to be a maker.

WEAVING A GRATEFUL HEART

Bio **:** Rina Matsumura is a tapestry weaver from Calgary, Alberta. She is a registered nurse who has worked in the field of mental health for more than fifteen years. Her woven wall hangings represent her passion for creativity and mental health advocacy.

Find more of her work on Instagram at @avelanewallart.

*S*howing pieces of me to the world, when words don't seem like enough—this is where my art takes over.

I've always had a love for craft and all things handmade. I witnessed my mother making beautiful things with her hands, and I got my desire to create from her. But this love turned into necessity as I searched for solace from my busy career as a mental health nurse and the day-to-day hustle of being a wife and a mother to two young boys. Mental fatigue was quickly turning into emotional exhaustion, and I needed a release; I needed freedom to let go of the things I could not change.

I started weaving in the summer of 2016, when I found a beginner frame loom weaving class at a local yarn store and signed up. It was love at first warp! Since that first class I have spent a lot of time experimenting, unraveling, and redoing to get to where I am now. I also make all of my looms myself, using the frames from art canvases, nails, and a hammer. People are often surprised when I tell them that I weave; I think there is a perception that this is an "old" craft, and I love the look of surprise when they see how it can translate to a modern, textured piece of art. For me, the beauty of weaving is in the unlimited creative opportunity. There are no limits or rules when it comes to creating something beautiful with fiber.

Weaving has become my self-care; it allows me the space to decompress from the hustles of daily life and to let go of the emotional burden of my nursing work, and a quiet place to practice mindfulness. As a mental health nurse, I have the privilege of hearing people's most intimate experiences, stories of their suffering, and I often carry the weight and gravity of their narratives with me. Recently, this past winter, a patient I had worked with closely and whom I had known for some time died by suicide, and it was heart-wrenching; the feelings of helplessness, despair, loss, and grief all came flooding in, along with feelings of guilt that took time to process. I don't talk about my patients' stories outside of work, out of respect for their privacy and confidentiality, but this makes it even more difficult to process all of my own thoughts and feelings when they arise.

Weaving has been my savior through the tough days and strong emotions. I can sit at the loom with tears streaming down my face, and somehow the sorrows of my patients, the pain I feel for their experiences, can be woven into the rhythmic under and over, under and over, until the universe starts to feel right again. Each row is woven with intention, with emotion, the process of releasing pain being transformed into something creative and beautiful.

Weaving has also helped me navigate my own personal experiences with anxiety. I have always been an introvert and have experienced social anxiety my entire life. Then, after my second son was hospitalized at three months old due to a life-threatening

medical situation, I began having panic attacks. As a mental health nurse, I felt I should have the knowledge of how to stop this, of how I could cope with my anxiety, but I was unable to get the worries out of my head. This is where weaving has continued to help me; it has created a space for me to be present, to focus on what I am doing in the moment and nothing else. I have been able to access gratitude—to turn my worries into appreciation for the good things and to be thankful for what I have right in front of me.

Pursuing my art has not been without challenges. As a wife and mother with a career outside of the home, finding time to weave has been a labor of love, my passion driving me to challenge the cynic inside me that says it is too hard. A majority of my time spent weaving is in the evening and on the weekends, the result being that I sacrifice time with my family. It's a willing sacrifice, for now, as I am a better person when I've had some time to create, to recharge, and to work on something I am passionate about. I will be the first to admit that I don't have it all figured out; each new day is a new learning opportunity on how to juggle it all.

I want my weaving to represent my passion for fiber art, as well as my dedication to mental health advocacy, as these two things are at the forefront of my heart, each inspiring and fueling the other. Avelane Wall Art was born through an earlier idea to write about mental health (I quickly realized that blogging was not my thing) on a blog called *Unravel and Reboot*, and the name Avelane, taken from "unrAVEL ANd rEboot," still holds the underpinnings of my original ideas around advocacy for better knowledge and education around mental health issues. Avelane

Wall Art represents my own journey with needing to unravel to make sense of my experiences, to then reboot to move forward with new perspective. I've also learned to appreciate that what I do as a nurse is a great privilege, and that being an advocate also means living a life that I encourage others to live.

In the final step of finishing each woven piece, I sew a little green heart into the lower right-hand corner, which represents the merging of my passions for art and mental health. Each piece that is sold has a portion given back to the community, through the purchasing and donation of items to help those in need and through various mental health initiatives. I feel grateful that creating art provides me with a vehicle to help others, to advocate for those who are still struggling to find their voice, and a platform to speak up and educate those around me about mental illness.

Weaving has given me joy along with comfort; it has been my refuge when the tides have been rough, when life throws things in my path that I cannot control or explain. It has taught me how to access the parts of myself I once struggled to connect with and has given me confidence that what I create is beautiful. Weaving has taught me gratitude, and I now take great pride in what I do. My weaving is an expression of who I am, the different parts of my identity, and how I have chosen to show and share myself with the world. Each of my woven pieces holds a story, but the end result is always a grateful heart.

A FUTURE
BIGGER THAN OURSELVES

Bio : Bethany and Rhys Evans-Brown are the cofounders of Woolberry Fiber Co., where they create small-batch, hand-dyed yarn inspired by nature, helping makers create a little more quiet in their busy lives. They have a young son, Theodore, who is in charge of quality control, making sure every skein is knit-worthy. They enjoy traveling, making sure to find the local yarn shop and coffee shop wherever they go.

You can find their yarn at woolberryfiberco.com and follow along with their journey on Instagram @woolberryfiberco.

Photography: Sam Ott-Grandlich

*I*f you asked me what the scariest thing I've ever done is, it's this—betting on myself to make my dreams a reality.

Rewind to four years ago: My husband, Rhys, and I were living in New Zealand. We were newly married and would spend the first few years of our marriage exploring this beautiful country. Rhys—a New Zealand native—wanted nothing more than for me to experience his home country, his culture, his family, before packing our lives into four tiny suitcases and boarding our plane back to the United States.

Our tiny one-bedroom apartment—a two-minute walk from the beach—was tightly nestled between beach homes and was where I would spend most of my time creating. My love for all things wool took shape here. In our bedroom, listening to podcasts and knitting alongside them; in our living room, learning to spin fiber gifted to me by my mother-in-law; in our kitchen, attempting to dye thrifted yarn with food coloring. This place allowed me time to reflect, focus, face fears, and begin the long journey of courage to become who I was created to be.

Our time in New Zealand came to an end, and after what felt like a whirlwind of emotions and countless phone calls to our immigration lawyer, we were seated on the plane, ready to begin the next chapter of our lives.

Reentering America, we felt out of place as we began navigating what life here could be. Rhys found a job at a local coffee shop, but I felt lost. I felt as if my spirit had come alive in New Zealand, creating and working with fiber, and I knew I couldn't let that feeling go, but I was terrified to fail. Then I remembered this quote printed on an air freshener that dangled from my rearview mirror, which I used to read almost every day on my way to work:

The future belongs to those who believe in the beauty of their dreams.

—Eleanor Roosevelt

I believed in the beauty of what my dream could be, but the courage to take that leap was where I was lacking. Thankfully, my husband saw that glimmer of courage hidden deep inside and knew that was all I needed to begin.

I spent months researching bases, dyes, packaging supplies, color concepts, dye methods, taxes, business licenses—everything I needed to create this business.

After what seemed like a never-ending list, I was finally ready for my first shop update, on October 14, 2016. I remember running around frantically, hoping I had prepared everything, switching between wondering whether anyone would even make a purchase and how I would actually fulfill each order—I was exhilarated. I never knew the joy that could come from simply sitting at my computer counting down the minutes until my first update was live. To be honest, I still get those butterflies today.

As the months flew by, this crazy dream began to take shape. The shop began to sell more, which meant I was able to purchase even more yarn for

each subsequent update. My husband began to work behind the scenes in the evenings after working full-time as a carpenter, helping dye yarn while I was pregnant with our son, and my mom graciously offered to pack orders when my stomach got too heavy for me to bend over anymore. I even went into labor while I was at the post office dropping off shop orders. Updates began flying by, and before we knew it, we had a beautiful baby boy, a sweet little apartment, and a giant dilemma—I couldn't maintain the business on my own. I was burnt out, exhausted, and stressed and had one too many emotional breakdowns to continue on alone.

We began chatting about what to do next. Our lives—a fleeting moment in time—seemed to be propelling us to this crossroads of trust or fear. We knew what we needed to do. However, Rhys had recently been promoted and was enjoying his job. After months of thoughtful discussion, we went in. All in. Rhys quit his job, and I threw him a "Welcome to the Business" party, complete with balloons, streamers, and homemade beignets.

We are now nearing one year as a small family business with Woolberry as our sole income. It is exhilarating, scary, inspiring, and humbling all in one breath. The thought that the dream I had could provide for my family is incredible. However, I knew our company needed to be more than just a provision for ourselves. Back at the beginning, while researching bases, dyes, and business licenses, something was missing. I knew no matter how small or big this business became, we needed a mission—a vision beyond ourselves.

So back in 2016, I started researching non-profit organizations and remembered that my sister had worked as a secretary for a nonprofit, Charity: Water. She had incredible memories from her time there, and I began searching through their website and researching their ethics; watching the videos of them building wells in remote villages and blessing these communities with fresh drinking water. It was inspiring, and I dreamed of what it would be like to help fund a well for a community. To provide them with clean water to prevent diseases and empowering girls and boys to spend their time gaining an education and build a fulfilling future for them and their families. To be a part of an organization that is reshaping the future.

This past December, our dream became a humbling reality. We were able to fund a water project through Charity: Water, building three wells in India. This isn't just our accomplishment, though; it is all of our customers. At the heart of our company, I knew I wanted our foundation to be firm, genuine, and authentic. My hope of donating 5 percent of our sales to go toward a well fund was never a ploy to gain more customers, but always a way for we who have resources and privileges to focus our energy on building others up.

We knew there was so much more to this business than just squishy yarn and a pretty Instagram feed. It is about building a community of makers who are passionate—passionate about their craft, about life, about the world, about encouraging and building up others' dreams. There are millions of makers in the world—each with their own unique story. Try betting on your dreams. Chances are you'll surprise even yourself.

THE PETITE KNITTER

Bio : Born in the tropics, Weichien Chan is a knitwear designer who now lives in the Canadian Arctic. Colorwork yoke sweaters are her favorite things to knit.

Follow her knitting journey on Instagram at @thepetiteknitter.

This series of photos is a collection of our lives in the northernmost territory in Canada. Some places in Canada, as well as the world, experience extremely low temperatures in winter, but none as long, unforgiving, and bitter as the Arctic winters. Northern realities often defy what most people consider "normal." Life above the tree line means we don't get to see the colors change in fall; nor do we get to smell spring when the trees bud. The vast tundra, with permafrost as ground, where vegetation is virtually nonexistent, however, takes on its own definition of beauty. Nature is so bizarre; it somehow finds ways to reward us for the long winters. Not only do we get twenty-four-hour daylight in summer, as long as the sun sets and the sky is clear, but the northern lights dance regardless of the time of year. This is what defines the Great White North. When life is so slow and quiet, these north-of-60 views are what feed my soul and ignite my creativity. But it's important to note the real struggles of remote living. Being on an Arctic island can mean no road access at times, as the ocean is frozen almost year-round. This comes with a long list of issues like food insecurities and lack of access to health care, to name a few. As with most things in life, there is so much more than what meets the eye, and that couldn't be more true when it comes to the Canadian Arctic.

MOMMY MAKER

Bio : Karina Agustina is the mind and soul behind missbananacrafts. Her designs are heavily influenced by "mom life" and her kids. She works on simple and daily-use projects, so that even very busy moms can still crochet for their kids and, of course, for themselves.

Find Karina's latest design updates on Instagram @missbananacrafts and her blog, www.missbananacrafts.com.

I was an architect in one of the largest architecture firms in Singapore. It felt like the busiest job in an incredibly busy city. I loved my life and my job, very much. But I got married, and practically, as for many women in Asia, it meant that my career was over. Then my whole world shifted again the second I had my first daughter. I barely had time for myself anymore. I was even busier than when I was an architect. I had zero time to focus on my well-being, zero time for creativity. I thought, *This is it*. It's the end of me as myself, and from that moment I would exist as "mom" or "wife" only. People would soon forget about Karina, the architect, the independent woman, the creative woman.

I don't mind being a wife and a mom; I am proud to be both. But deep down inside, I was longing for an identity people would recognize me for, a trait of *myself* people would acknowledge. But I hate it when people asked what my job was and looked down on me when I answered, "A housewife." A housewife is not an easy job. We have constant work to do, have huge responsibilities—not to mention those who are also parents and raise human beings! But in between the limited amount of time and energy I had, I still wanted a way to look at myself and feel proud of me. I found a strand of hope within crafting, specifically crochet.

I spent a lot of my childhood in my grandma's house; she was a seamstress, a knitter, and also a crocheter. She taught me the basic skills of sewing and crocheting, but I didn't really put those skills into practice until recently. I was pregnant with Rinn when I bumped into a cute amigurumi book while waiting to catch a flight. It really spoke to the crafter within my soul. *Whoa, you can make these cute dolls with crochet?* It was a simple thought, but I hadn't used a crochet hook since I was that little girl, let alone read a pattern. How in the world could I decipher this confusing language? It was finally time to board my flight, and I was still considering whether to buy the book or not. I looked at the tutorial section . . . *I think I can recognize some of the techniques.* Well, so be it. I bought the book and hunted for the tools and materials needed.

Through much trial and error, I finally learned the right way to create amigurumi, and I started to feel I had found a new identity for myself as a crocheter. I soon became a toy maker, who "upgraded" amigurumi patterns into a rattle, a teether, a mobile—anything related to babies. But never once did I think I could design my own amigurumi, until I realized I could make the pattern so much easier to read, so much quicker to do, since time is very scarce for a new mom.

I designed my first amigurumi, Ballerina Rabbit, to be made with minimal seams; the only things you need to sew are the arms and ears. I was very pleased with it, and it didn't take long for me to start designing

more patterns. After amigurumi, I took an interest in kids' clothing. Why? Because it was so dang cute to see my babies in something I had made. (And because kids' wearables are smaller, and therefore take less time to make and use less material.)

Along the way, I met so many amazing designers and makers online. And I realized that what I am doing is what I was looking for all along—a way to love myself and an identity for myself. Crafting made me feel content. But none of this would have happened if I hadn't become a mother. I wouldn't have picked up that crochet hook if I hadn't wanted to make amigurumi for my baby. I wouldn't know the wonders of crochet if not for my children. All my designs are based on my daughters, be it their favorite animals, their toys, their clothes. In the end, my children draw out the best in me—they're not an obstacle in my life; they're gigantic gifts God sent me.

If you're a woman and a passionate crafter, possibly on your way to building a family, embrace it. It will take a whole lot of investment, time, and energy, but it may all be worth it, much like being a maker. You may worry that life is practically over the moment you have a child. And I know most makers are afraid to lose their time for making. But the creative soul inside every one of us can thrive alongside parenting or any relationship or endeavor; we only need to be more creative in how we balance our passions. Place your family in the spotlight; use them as your inspirations. But never stop making; never stop being a maker.

DENIM AND RAIN

Bio: Sarah Bronske is the designer, maker, artist, and photographer behind Denim and Rain. Being a part-time stay-at-home mom and small-business owner, she always keeps busy and thrives when active.

You can find her on Instagram as @denim.and.rain.fibers.

I wanted to share a glimpse into my world of making in my home. I do have to admit, though, that this is a very small and clean look into it. I promise you that behind the camera was a pile of laundry and two kids who were making a mess of the place. Those two kids are the reason I started it all, though, so I will happily allow the messes while I work. Five years ago I made a bear hood for my daughter and was convinced to open a shop to sell them, so I did, and it was okay. I didn't sell out overnight or anything, but it brought in a little extra money so I could buy clothes for the kids and more yarn. Over time my business evolved; I now write patterns for garments and dye yarn. If you'd told me that when I started, I would have laughed at the idea.

No matter how much things change, though, the one consistency through the years has been that I do what I love. I have told myself that I will never force myself to make anything I don't enjoy. If I feel like dyeing yarn, I will go for it; if I hate a pattern that I'm writing, I will put it away until I am inspired again. Now if only I could do that with the housework . . .

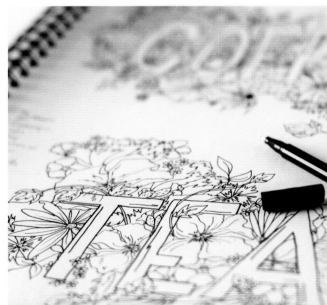

CHOOSE THE WONDERFUL

Bio : Janine Myska is a knit and crochet designer from Winnipeg, Canada. She loves sunshine, laughter, and craft beer. She lives in Alberta with her partner, Matt, and their two huskies, Pancake and Hudson.

Visit her blog at www.knitsnknots.ca for knit and crochet patterns and inspiration.

Photography: Stephanie Penner

I have always been an extremely optimistic person. My high school graduation quote was something like, "When you learn to see the beauty in all things, people see the beauty in you." I chose this because as I was growing up, I discovered that I was especially drawn to positive people who understood that life was a mixed bag of wonderful and awful, but who chose to focus on the wonderful. So many things make this life worth living; one is the ability to create.

I have expressed myself in creative ways for as long as I can remember. My childhood consisted of art classes, sewing lessons, piano lessons, arts and crafts in the kitchen with Play-Doh, pipe cleaners, beads. . . . My parents must have wondered where my "off" button was, because I was constantly asking questions about anything and everything. Each answer led only to more questions. There has always been a curiosity in me that could never be quenched.

There was a period in my life during university when I put my hobbies aside to focus on school and work, and not much else. I dreaded being asked to "tell me about yourself," because I didn't really love to do much of anything. I had so many interests when I was young, but as I grew into an adult, I left them behind. And then at nineteen I lost my dad unexpectedly. This was the man who sat through every gymnastics practice and every art class, and took me shopping at the fabric store before every sewing les-son. He always encouraged his daughters to try new things, and I think my thirst for life largely comes from his influence. This loss put life into perspective as we struggled to readjust as a family of three.

Life threw me a curveball. Things were now colorless, mundane, and depressing. I missed my old life. I knew there was nothing I could change about what happened, but I could change the way I let it affect me. I wanted to transform those feelings of sadness into something productive. I wanted to re-acquaint myself with my creativity, because I needed an outlet. I wanted to find something that I loved to do—something that was just for me. Something that could distract me. Something I could get lost in.

The next Christmas, my mom gave me a round knitting loom and a ball of yarn. Shortly afterward, our apartment was overtaken with yarn and more hats than I could wear. I started selling them online under the name "Knits 'N Knots." This was a new-to-me craft, but it gave me a familiar feeling. I could feel my old self coming back, bubbly and optimistic as ever.

It wasn't until I taught myself to crochet and knit that I became completely obsessed. I found myself lying in bed every night, unable to sleep, because I wanted to keep knitting or to try the latest stitch I had learned. I was mesmerized by the way intricate fabric could be created with just needles and yarn. I would dream of hats, yarn, and color combinations. I was immersed into this brand-new world that I just could not get enough of.

At this point, I was graduating with a degree in a field I was no longer interested in. My heart was no longer in it; it was all tangled up in the fiber arts. For the next couple of years, every second of my time was spent on Knits 'N Knots, trying my best to make it into something I could do long-term, to prove to everyone that it was possible to make a career out of knitting and crocheting, and to prove to myself that I could do it. I dropped out of a master's degree program to pursue knitting and crochet—you can imagine the concerned looks on people's faces when I told them. Truthfully, I had no idea what I was doing most of the time, but losing a parent made me realize that life is too short not to try.

When I'm making something new, I feel as if I am transforming my thoughts, my energy, my personality, and my experiences into something tangible. Each piece I have designed is tied to a memory or a feeling. I remember exactly what I was doing at that time or what was going on in my life. One of my favorite designs is a crocheted vest that I made in the summer of 2017. I wore it to an event in Toronto where I got to meet a lot of my maker friends for the first time. It was also the first piece that introduced me to the world of pattern writing. My bralettes remind me of sitting on my deck with a gin and tonic in the sunshine, chatting with my mom as she gardened beside me. My first time learning the long-tail cast-on method was during spring break of 2016, when my boyfriend went out with his friends but I stayed home, determined to learn this technique. One of my hats reminds me of knitting on the floor in my family room and binge-watching *Game of Thrones* until four in the morning as I worked late nights during the Christmas season. I am not *just* knitting, *just* crocheting. Each piece is special, a glimpse into what my life was like at the time of creating it. It is not only about the finished product, but about the process and what that process brings me mentally, spiritually, and emotionally.

My dad passed away before I ever picked up a crochet hook or knitting needles, but he had the strongest influence on my maker story out of anyone in my life. He had a lot of interesting hobbies and was always willing to try new things. He understood the importance of finding something you love to do, not just to gain a new skill but to *feed your soul*. He never told me this word-for-word, but he showed me by example, and I'm still thankful that I was paying attention.

When I first discovered the fiber arts, I remember thinking how magical it was that something beautiful could be created with just a string and a hook. I still feel that same excitement every time I pick up a project. I get to create something today that didn't exist yesterday. Even though I know the world is a mixed bag of wonderful and awful, I will spend the rest of my life focusing on the wonderful.

FOLK & FIBRE CO.

Bio : Ashley is the designer and creator behind Folk & Fibre Co., a shop dedicated to supplying makers with accessories, patterns, and yarn that are both modern and timeless. You'll never find her without her project bag and whatever new design is in the works. Her dream is to someday have her own downtown studio/creative space somewhere in northeastern Wisconsin, but for now, as a mom of two, she loves the flexibility of being able to work from home and snuggle her little ones whenever she can.

For your daily dose of yarn and inspiration, follow Ashley on Instagram at @folkandfibreco.

*F*iber can be so fragile. Bare unspun wool is delicate, easily torn, and tangled. Its shape and form are manipulated with little effort. But once that wool has been drafted and wound, spun, and plied, it becomes much stronger, reliable in its shape and texture, and not so easily broken.

This feels like the mind of a maker to me. We begin our journeys in a place that is so unsure, with little know-how but dreaming big dreams of where these skills can take us. It becomes easy for us to fall for the lies that tell us where we need to be, and we forget the truths of where we are. We are still easily manipulated and swayed one way or the other by what we read on the internet or by what we see others accomplishing; instead of finding contentment in our current state we long to reach those milestones that others have reached. Creating itself is a process; it literally means "to bring something into existence." Something that doesn't just happen overnight.

There are so many skills to be taught, tools to discover, and people to learn from. Remember, this is a part of everyone's story. Every skein must first be spun.

These photos are a glimpse into where I am finding joy in my maker life during this chapter of my story. Life is almost never stress free (most of the time I'm an emotional mess), but inspiration can even be found in the messiest corners of life. When we can't find the strength to creatively show up, there's always someone who is showing up for us (paraphrased from Psalm 46:1–3).

KENYARN

Bio : Jake Kenyon grew up in a small town in southeastern Massachusetts and currently resides in a tiny studio in Providence, Rhode Island. In his day-to-day life as a speech-language pathologist, Jake wears only a few different-colored scrubs while working, but he's always noticing the colors in the bouquet on a patient's bedside table or distinct color patterns in the New England foliage. He spends his days off washing, dyeing, skeining, and writing patterns. Kenyarn is where Jake shares his perspective on the beauty in the world around us through hand-dyed yarn.

To shop Jake's hand-dyed fiber, visit Kenyarn.com or find him on Instagram @isthatkenyarn.

Photography: Hannah Marlin

*D*yeing yarn is about finding the magic in the world and bringing it to life with color. It's about turning emotion into color. Holding a colorway is about more than just how it feels in your hands; it's about how it makes you feel in your heart.

When friends ask how I come up with colorways, I reply, "It's simple—find what you love and make it your palette." For me, those interests are the more magical aspects of our world: astrology, Tarot, and crystals, which I often turn to for inspiration.

The thing about being a maker is that no one can define you. It's about inventing yourself and stepping away from what is "safe." Every day becomes an adventure about what new and exciting project I can tackle or how I can turn the ordinary into the extraordinary. For me, this craft is about finding a balance between opening up emotionally and escaping from the daily grind, as well as using making to foster and create connections across this community.

Submerge yourself in your passion. Spend time with your craft and keep the dialogue with your craft open. Sometimes the most unexpected of roadblocks are really just stepping-stones leading you down the path that was meant for you. Keep an open mind, and the possibilities are endless.

JOURNEY TO DYEING

Bio : Jennifer Sylvester is the indie dyer and slow knitter behind Laine & Lotus Fiber Co., a New England–based shop featuring small-batch hand-dyed yarn. Her love of fiber arts is ever expanding, and she truly feels she was meant to express her creative soul through her hand-dyed yarn. Her other passions include coffee, chocolate, Netflix, and her sweet little family.

Her yarn can be found online at www.laineandlotus.com.

*L*ike many other makers, my introduction to the fiber world came at a time when I was feeling lost. Don't get me wrong, I was in a great place in my life. I had just had my son, we had just bought our first family home, and the love and support I received from my partner to stay home and raise our child rather than returning to my day job were something I never thought I'd have, and I am beyond grateful for that. But being a stay-at-home mom is *hard*. Like, really, really *hard*. The hardest, most rewarding job I've ever had. And sometimes it's difficult not to lose yourself to the identity of "Momma."

It was October and my man was away on business. I remember seeing a video on Facebook about a DIY arm-knit infinity scarf. You may have seen it. It looked pretty and easy enough. I went to my local JOANN, picked up some Thick & Quick, and decided to try it while my son napped that afternoon. I cannot lie; it took me a good two or three times to get it right, but once it was finally done I was actually happy with it. I made another, then another, and a few more before having an epiphany—if I can arm knit, what's stopping me from actually knitting with needles?

My grandmother was an avid knitter and crocheter. I remember always having a crocheted granny-square blanket at the end of my bed growing up. As a child, I used to weave pieces of yarn in and out of the holes, pretending that I was crocheting. My mother has always been crafty as well, quilting, sewing, painting, and doing a bit of the fiber arts, too. My sister is a scrapbooker and a beautiful cake artist.

My brother is a builder and literally constructs homes where there was once nothing. . . . Me? I was never much of a creative. As much as I wanted to be good at it, art was never really my strong suit.

After those initial projects, I called my mom and asked if she had any spare hooks, needles, or yarn hanging around that I could practice with. She gladly brought me over a care package. In it, she had yarn from her stash, some straight needles, and a faded blue cigar tube filled with my grandmother's old crochet hooks. My grandmother, who was my namesake, and I had been very close prior to her passing in my early teens, and just holding her hooks in my hand instantaneously made me feel connected to her once again.

My mom showed me a few stitches of each craft, and I turned to YouTube for the rest. In the beginning, I caught on to crochet much more easily than knitting, so I decided that was where I would place my focus. Before I knew it, I was making things. Like, real, legitimate things. Were they good? Heck no! But they were items that *I made* with yarn and a hook. Even now, to stop and think about that amazes me.

With practice I got better, and I started sharing what I was making with my friends and family. It took me by complete surprise when people wanted to start buying the things I was making. It filled me with pride, accomplishment, and a ton of anxiety. *What if they are disappointed with my work? What if it doesn't fit? What if it falls apart?* The self-doubt was loud and echoing, but the prospect of finding

a way to start financially contributing to my family again was enough to push me through that noise in my head.

When I gained a bit more confidence in myself and my craft, I asked around for ways to spread the word about my makes. A longtime friend suggested Instagram, and although I had zero idea how an Instagram account was going to help grow my business, I followed his advice. To this day I have yet to thank him for opening me up to the amazing fiber community that exists in the Instagram world. (So hey, Timmy B., if you're reading this: thank you!)

One of the very first true connections I made on Instagram is actually the first person who piqued my interest in yarn dyeing. One day she posted about yarn she had hand dyed, and the yarn posts kept on coming. What? I bought yarn at my local JOANN or Michaels, and that's what yarn was to me. Most of the people I followed on Instagram used commercial yarns as well, but to see the colors she created on yarn herself had my head spinning. How was that even possible? What was this magic??

I thought about how amazing it would be to dye my own yarn, but I had no idea where to start. The self-doubt set in again. I was finally starting to pave a path of quality modern crochet and knitwear. I was becoming known for the makes I put out, and I didn't want to shake the foundation I had worked so hard to build. *There's no way you can dye yarn, stay in your lane*. And that was that.

But my eyes had been opened to this amazing world of indie-dyed yarn, and I couldn't just ignore it. I started finding more and more dyers on Instagram, and every once in a while I would feel extra inspired and start researching the process of dyeing. The fiber, the pans, the heat source, the dyes, the drying, the space you need to accomplish it all . . . *nope, you can't do it, focus on what you're doing*. Which, at the time, was making. Day in and day out, making.

When things finally did calm down that spring, I attended Stitches United with one of the best real-life friends I have made from the fiber community on Instagram. Walking around squeezing, seeing, touching, smelling, and just taking in the beauty of all of the hand-dyed yarn at the event was what it took to push me over the edge. By this time it had been years since I first toyed with the idea of dyeing. For *years* I had been making one excuse after another as to why I couldn't try to dye my own yarn. But after Stitches I threw all the excuses out the window. I went home and immediately dove into researching everything I could about dyeing. I ordered a small dyeing kit that came with yarn, dye, and a few tools, and I ordered a pot to use for my dyeing experiments. I went to my local library and took out all the books they had on yarn dyeing. I read them and took notes. I watched video after video on YouTube. I read tutorials and watched videos on dyers' IG feeds. After all that, I tried to dye my first skein.

I had a very specific vision in my head of what I wanted my skein to look like—a vision that was blown out of the water almost immediately after the dye hit the yarn. This was going to take some practice. Although my first skein didn't come out the way I had envisioned it, I didn't hate it. I would try a different technique next time. Next time came, and another vision was completely undone by the organic nature of the dye's interaction with the water and the yarn. As I stepped into this new craft I lacked control, and that was extremely hard for me.

I continued to experiment, and after every time I found myself saying, "It isn't exactly what I envisioned, but I like it," so I decided to embrace my inner Elsa and try to (gasp!) let go a bit. I started going into my dye sessions with fewer expectations and looser visions. I tried to start embracing the organic nature of the dye, to work with it instead of trying to control it. Through a lot of trial and error, I began to learn how and why certain things occur during dye sessions. I was feeling more comfortable in the studio. It was time to share my beauties with the world.

April 9, 2018, was my first post to Instagram featuring my hand-dyed yarn. That skein of yarn sold within minutes, with several inquiries from my followers as to whether or not I would have any more available for purchase. This felt good. It felt right. It was then that I decided to transition my business— or at least try. I was going to jump in feet-first. My feed went from a steady stream of images of cozy knits and WIPs to mostly photos of skeins of yarn. My first official shop update was more successful than I could have hoped. The support and encouragement I received from the maker community was beyond heartwarming, and more than anything, it was validating.

Soon I rebranded. I created a website. I hit milestones and started collaborations that had once been a distant dream. I still have many goals to achieve, but I would be lying if I said I wasn't proud of how far I've come. From the very beginning, I took a chance. I stuck with it even though it was a challenge for my personality, and very different from what I was used to. I listened to my heart, to my creative soul. And it was one of the best things I ever could have done.

VANESSA BARRAGÃO

Bio : Studio Vanessa Barragão is a design studio focusing on using artisanal techniques and wasted yarns from the industry to produce textiles and products for interiors. Vanessa's work is inspired by coral reefs' environments, cleverly combining craft and recycled materials into unique and luxurious sculptural carpets and tapestries for floors and walls. Licensed and with a master's degree in fashion and textile design, she's based in Porto, Portugal, and divides her time between collaborating as a textile designer for an artisanal rugs factory and running her studio.

Visit her online at vanessabarragao.com and @vanessabarragao_work.

HOW LETTING GO OF DOUBT AND PERFECTION MEANT EVERYTHING

Bio : Megan Shaimes is the owner of Megmade with Love, a crochet blog that features simple and stylish crochet patterns—clothing, accessories, and home decor. It's her mission to show you how to crochet stuff you'd be proud to show off.

Visit megmadewithlove.com for free patterns, inspiration, and crochet-related articles.

I've never failed to get in the way of myself each and every time I've wanted to do something big with my life, especially when it came to owning a business. There's this part of me that has crazy amazing dreams and aspirations, and I love this side of myself. It's like I'm a little kid again, and anything is possible when I start dreaming of what I can do with my talents and creativity. I call this part of me "Innocent Little Dreamer."

Then there's the self-sabotaging part of me. It's the boring, scared, grown-up version of myself that I honestly don't love; we'll call her "The Doubter." The Doubter takes a look at what Innocent Little Dreamer has schemed up and laughs in her face. *Wait, you think you're gonna do that?* she always seems to say condescendingly. And before Innocent Little Dreamer can even think of a rebuttal, in floods even more doubt. *This isn't possible for you. Someone like her can do it, but certainly not you. . . . You don't even have the abilities or resources to take that on! You'd never find the time, and you're not even organized enough to see it through. . . . You don't want to look like an idiot, do you?* Kinda brutal, right?

There have been times when I've mustered up the strength to ignore what The Doubter had to say. One such time was starting a photography business, and another was a wooden sign-making business. And each time I managed to get past The Doubter it was because I was able to laser focus on the result that my goal or dream business would provide for me. I wanted to express myself creatively, connect with

people through that, and earn money from it—and these dreams could take me there! I wish I could say this was the successful end for my first two business ideas, but getting past The Doubter wasn't enough, because I ultimately ran into another voice—and that one's name was "Fearful Perfectionist."

Fearful Perfectionist was the type of gal who cared a great deal about what people thought of her work. She took my once-achievable dreams and goals and made them seem impossible, because there was so much work to be done—and the work had to be perfect, after all. She helped ease me into the comfy spot of mediocrity, because the risk of a grand dream was all too overwhelming. And dare I mention the *f* word? Yup, *failure* was one she always threw my way. And sadly, Fearful Perfectionist was a big reason both of those businesses didn't thrive. I look back and think about how I could have done so much more with each of those ideas, yet I let them both fizzle out. I dropped the ball and let the fear of going all in affect my work.

So when it came to my current business, Megmade with Love, of course The Doubter and Fearful Perfectionist made their expected appearances. I heard all the same old things from them again, yet this time I was armed with knowledge from my past ventures. Plus, I was extra motivated to make this business work, because I wanted to earn income and stay home with my son, Sawyer. I knew how to get past The Doubter like I had before in my previous businesses, but then there was still Fearful Perfectionist to

deal with. But this time I made a commitment to post content to my website consistently for an entire year and promised myself that if by the end of the year I didn't enjoy doing it, or if it didn't take off, I could quit. And if I came to the end of that year making money and thriving creatively, then jackpot! At least I could say I put in my all. And you know what? That shut Fearful Perfectionist right up.

I learned a lot that first year about business—showing up week in and week out. I learned that the "start" of my business actually wasn't as big of a deal as I thought. It was only a small speck of all the work I would put into it. And it makes me wonder how many people are also hindered by the idea of starting. I could totally see The Doubter feeding us this lie. The big difference between someone who is living out their big dream and another who is unhappily sitting on their couch wishing *they* were achieving their

dream is that the first person took the plunge without knowing every little thing. And I'm going to bet they probably did it despite feeling scared.

I will say my life isn't entirely a walk in the park now that I'm actually running my business and chasing my dreams. Fearful Perfectionist and The Doubter still make appearances from time to time. Anytime I sense Fearful Perfectionist heading my way with a shame-filled statement, I've learned it's best combated with a plunge into action. No way am I always perfect at fighting it, though; of course I can fall into their traps from time to time—I'm only human. But while I'm tempted to listen to the "I told you so" that's in the back of my mind, I simply choose to get up, dust off my pants, and get back into the game with a different strategy. I think Innocent Little Dreamer would be proud, don't you?

ALIMARAVILLAS

Bio : Alicia Recio is a nursery school director, crochet designer, sneaker enthusiast, and yarnbomber.

Follow her journeys online at alimaravillas.es and @alimaravillas.

I am passionate about sneakers and yarn skeins. I like to investigate, discover, and learn about them. Collecting them, storing them visually, decorating my home, and creating a file about them is my way of channeling this passion and making my collections feel unique to me.

For each pair of shoes that I collect, I match it with a yarn ball, based on their color and qualities. Thus, through my peculiar way of communicating, the story behind the shoes and the characteristics of the yarns come through. This search for art has led me to know all kinds of brands of yarn and the different ideas that come out each season. So much so that I've been asked to be an advisor on what types of threads designers should use for projects.

It is in this way that my passion has become my way of life. I truly enjoy wearing a pair of sneakers at a game that's connected with the project that I am crocheting. To go outside myself and watch how they come together is my joy.

PART TWO

patterns

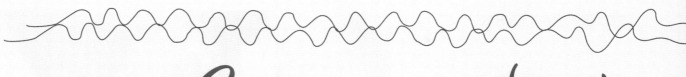

Cornerstone Scarf

Designed by Jewell Washington
of NorthKnits

FINISHED MEASUREMENTS
8½" (21.5 cm) wide and 65"
(165 cm) long

YARN
We Are Knitters The Petite Wool
(100% wool; 153 yards [140 m]
per 3½ oz [100 g] ball): 4 balls in
Natural

NEEDLES
Size US 11 (8 mm) straight
needles

GAUGE
9 sts and 12 rows = 4" (10 cm)

NOTE
This pattern calls for knitting
in a herringbone stitch over a
two-row repeat. While there
are multiple ways to specifically
achieve herringbone, this is
how I do it to achieve the scarf's
look. As you knit, you'll notice
the WS is bumpy while the RS
has a beautiful herringbone
zigzag texture.

SCARF PATTERN

CO 40 sts.

Row 1: *K1, sl1knitwise, k1, insert left needle into slipped st and lift it over the knit st and onto the left needle, insert right needle into the slipped st tbl, wrap the yarn, pull it through, and complete as you would a regular knit st; rep from * to end of row.

Row 2 (WS): *P2tog (but don't slip sts off left needle), purl into first st on left needle again, sl both sts off left needle; rep from * to end of row.

Rep Rows 1 and 2 until you reach Row 204, or until scarf measures 65" (165 cm) long.

BO.

FINISHING
Weave in ends.

Ramble Ridge Pullover

Designed by Holly Minton of Carpe Lana

Photography by TabiLynn Photography

SIZES
S (M, L, XL)

FINISHED MEASUREMENTS
34 (38, 42, 46)" [86 (96.5, 106.5, 117) cm] bust

YARN
Monsoon Calamity Moca Cotton Fingering (100% cotton; comes in different-size cones): 1,250 (1,325, 1,425, 1,495) yards #0043 Pale Green Stone Heather (MC) and 45–50 yards Light Grey (CC)

NEEDLES
Size US 7 (4.5 mm) 28" (71 cm) or 32" (81 cm) circular
Size US 5 (3.75 mm) 16" (40.5 cm) circular
Or size needed to obtain gauge

NOTIONS
Stitch holders

GAUGE
19 sts and 30 rows = 4" (10 cm) in garter stitch with larger needle

NOTES
- Gauge for this pattern changes considerably after blocking; block swatch prior to measuring gauge to achieve correct sizing.
- Pattern is designed for 2–4" (5–10 cm) positive ease.

PULLOVER PATTERN

SLEEVE 1

With larger needle and MC, and using provisional CO (see page 166), CO 34 (38, 38, 42) sts. Knit 10 (10, 12, 12) rows.

*Next row: K2, kfb, k until 3 sts remain, kfb, k2.
Knit 5 rows.
Repeat from * until there are 74 (78, 78, 84) sts.

Next row: K2, kfb, k until there are 3 sts, kfb, k2—76 (80, 80, 86) sts. Knit 5 (11, 17, 11) rows.

SHOULDER 1

Using cable CO, CO 78 sts—154 (158, 158, 164) sts.

Row 1: K across new sts and sleeve sts, CO 78 sts at end of row—232 (236, 236, 242) sts. Knit across all sts for 30 (38, 45, 53) rows.

K116 (118, 118, 121). Place remaining 116 (118, 118, 121) sts on a holder for Back Panel.

FRONT PANEL

Rows 1–67: Knit across. Place Front Panel sts on holder.

BACK PANEL

Return Back Panel sts to needle.
Rows 1–67: K across.

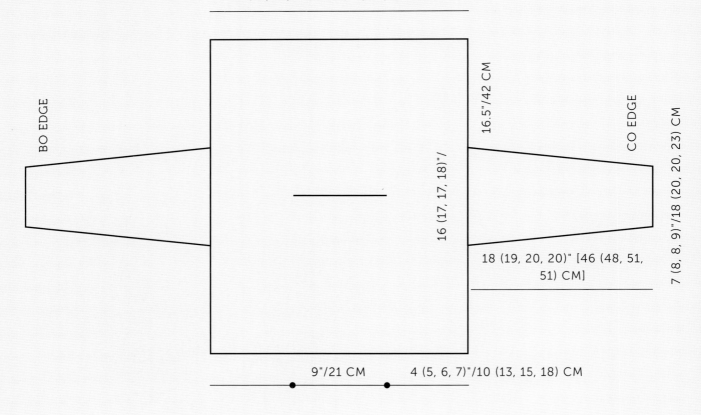

17 (19, 21, 23)"/43 (48, 53, 58.5) CM

BO EDGE

16.5"/42 CM

16 (17, 17, 18)"/

CO EDGE

7 (8, 8, 9)"/18 (20, 20, 23) CM

18 (19, 20, 20)" [46 (48, 51, 51) CM]

9"/21 CM   4 (5, 6, 7)"/10 (13, 15, 18) CM

SHOULDER 2

Return Front Panel sts to needle.
Knit across all sts for 30 (38, 45,
53) rows—232 (236, 236, 242) sts.
BO 78 sts; k remaining 154 (158,
158, 164) sts.
BO 78 sts; k remaining 76 (80,
80, 86) sts.

SLEEVE 2

Knit 5 (11, 17, 11) rows.
***Next row:** K2, k2tog, k until 4 sts
remain, k2tog, k2.
Knit 5 rows.
Repeat from * until 34 (38, 38,
42) sts remain.
Knit 10 (10, 12, 12) rows.
Switch to smaller needle and CC.
(K1, p1) across for 5 rows.
BO loosely.

SLEEVE 1 CUFF

Pick up Sleeve 1 sts from
provisional CO. With smaller
needle and CC:
K1, p1 for 5 rows.
BO loosely.

FINISHING

NECKLINE

With smaller needle and CC, pick
up an even number of sts evenly
around neckline opening.
(K1, p1) across for 5 rnds.
BO loosely.
Block garment to size. Seam
sides and sleeves. Weave in ends.

Favorite Cable Headband

Designed by Lindsey Faciane of
The Chesapeake Needle

FINISHED MEASUREMENTS
5½" (14 cm) wide and 22" (56 cm)
long

YARN
Lion Brand Yarn Vanna's Choice
(92% acrylic, 8% rayon; 145 yards
[133 m] per 3 oz [85 g] skein): 1
skein #403 Barley

NEEDLES
Size US 8 (5 mm)
Or size needed to obtain gauge

NOTIONS
Cable needle

GAUGE
17 sts and 24 rows = 4" (10 cm) in
Stockinette stitch

SPECIAL STITCH

Front Cross (FC): Work to the cabling section, as shown in **Photo A**. Next, place the specified number of stitches on your cable needle, as shown in **Photo B** (i.e., to work an FC4, you will place the next 4 stitches onto your cable needle). Holding the cable needle with the stitches in front of your work, knit the rest of the stitches in the cable section, as shown in **Photo C** (i.e., for an FC4, you will knit the next 4 stitches). Move the stitches on your cable needle to the edge of the needle, then knit the stitches off the cable needle, as shown in **Photo D**. Now your front cross cable is complete, as shown in **Photo E**.

B

A

C

D

E

HEADBAND PATTERN

CO 24 sts.

Row 1 and all WS (odd-numbered) rows: K2, p4, k2, p8, k2, p4, k2.

Row 2 (RS): K6, p2, k8, p2, k6.

Row 4: K6, p2, k8, p2, k6.

Row 6: K2, FC2, p2, k8, p2, FC2, k2.

Row 8: K6, p2, k8, p2, k6.

Row 10: K6, p2, k8, p2, k6.

Row 12: K2, FC2, p2, k8, p2, FC2, k2.

Row 14: K6, p2, k8, p2, k6.

Row 16: K6, p2, k8, p2, k6.

Row 18: K6, p2, FC4, p2, k6.

Repeat Rows 1–18 six more times, ending on Row 17 on the final repeat.

BO all sts. Work should measure approx. 22" (56 cm) long.

FINISHING

Block headband. Sew ends together. Weave in ends.

Itty Bitty Raglan

Designed by Christie Bodden
Photography by Madeleine
Chambers

SIZE
Newborn (0–12 months, 1 year,
2 years, 3 years)

FINISHED MEASUREMENTS
16 (19½, 21¾, 25, 27½)" [40.5
(49.5, 55, 63.5, 70) cm] chest

YARN
Berroco Vintage Chunky (52%
acrylic, 40% wool, 8% nylon; 136
yards [124 m] per 3½ oz [100 g]
hank)): 1 (2, 2, 3, 3) 3½ oz (100 g)
hanks #6105 Oats

NEEDLES
Size US 8 (5 mm) 16" (40.5 cm)
circular and set of double-
pointed needles
Size US 10 (6 mm) 16" (40.5 cm)
and 24" (61 cm) circular and set
of double-pointed needles

NOTIONS
Stitch markers
Waste yarn

GAUGE
14 sts and 21 rows = 4" (10 cm)
in Garter stitch with larger
needles

NOTE
This sweater is worked in the
round from the top down.

SWEATER PATTERN

COLLAR

With smaller 16" (40.5 cm) needles or dpns, CO 40 (48, 52, 52, 52) sts using the German Twisted CO Method or a stretchy CO method of your choice. Join and pm at BOR.

Rnd 1: *K1, p1; rep from * around.
Rep Rnd 1 four (six, six, six, eight) times.

RAGLAN SHAPING

Switch to larger needles.
Setup rnd: P6 (7, 7, 7, 7), pm, p8 (10, 12, 12, 12), pm, p12 (14, 14, 14, 14), pm, p8 (10, 12, 12, 12), pm, p6 (7, 7, 7, 7) to BOR (this will be the center back).
Rnd 1: *K to 1 st before marker, kfb, sm, k1, kfb; rep from * three more times, k to BOR—8 sts inc.
Rnd 2: Purl all sts.
Rep Rnds 1 and 2 five (seven, nine, eleven, thirteen) times—88 (112, 132, 148, 164) sts.

SEPARATE BODY AND SLEEVES

Sleeve setup rnd: *K to marker, remove marker, place 20 (26, 32, 36, 40) sleeve sts on a piece of waste yarn, CO 4 (4, 4, 6, 6) sts for underarm, remove marker; rep from * once more and knit to BOR—56 (68, 76, 88, 96) body sts.
Next rnd: Purl.
Next rnd: Knit.
Cont to work in Garter st until piece is 6 (8, 9, 10, 11)" [15 (20, 23, 25, 28) cm] long from collar CO edge.
Switch to smaller needles and work in 1x1 ribbing (k1, p1) for 4 (6, 8, 8, 8) rnds.
BO loosely.

SLEEVES

Transfer sleeve sts onto dpns or circular needle. Join yarn to work in the rnd.
Setup rnd: Starting at center of cast-on stitches at underarm, pick up and purl 2 (2, 2, 3, 3) underarm sts, purl around to last sleeve st, pick up and purl 2 (2, 2, 3, 3) underarm sts, pm to mark BOR.
Next rnd: Knit.
Next rnd: Purl.
Cont in garter st until piece is 5 (7, 8, 9, 10)" [13 (18, 20, 23, 25) cm] from picked-up edge of sleeve.
Dec rnd: K1, k2tog, k to last 3 sts, ssk, k1—18 (24, 30, 34, 38) sts.
Switch to smaller dpns. Work in 1x1 ribbing (k1, p1) for 4 (6, 8, 8, 8) rnds.
BO loosely in rib.

FINISHING

Weave in ends.

Generations Hat

Designed by Marlee Galina of MbyMKnitwear

SIZE

Fits most adults
Finished Measurements
8" (20.25 cm) tall (with regular brim) and 18" (45.5 cm) in circumference unstretched

YARN

BC Garn Semilla (100% organic wool; 175 yards [160 meters] per 1¾ oz [50 g] ball): 1 ball each #OB01 (MC), #OB101 (C1), #OB105 (C2), and #OB107 (C3)
Willow & Lark Plume (70% mohair, 30% silk; 229 yards [210 m] per .9 oz [25 g] ball): 1 ball each #300 Snow Drop (MC), #304 Heron Grey (C1), and #309 Tea Rose (C2)
Scheepjes Mohair Rhythm (70% mohair, 30% microfiber; 219 yards [200 m] per .9 oz [25 g] ball): 1 ball #688 Disco (C3)

NEEDLES

Size US 7 (4.5 mm) 16" (40.5 cm) circular
Size US 7 (4.5 mm) double-pointed needles
Size US 6 (4.0 mm) 16" (40.5 cm) circular
Or size needed to obtain gauge

NOTIONS

Stitch markers
Faux-fur pompom

GAUGE

24 sts and 25 rows = 4" (10 cm) in Stockinette stitch with larger needle and one strand each DK and laceweight held together

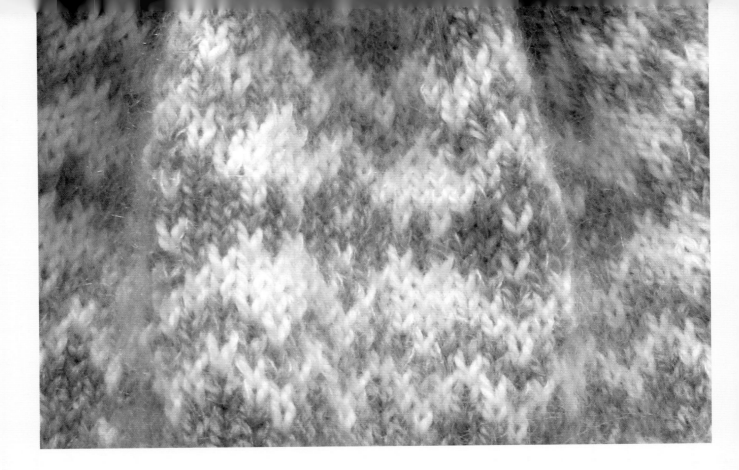

NOTES

Tips for Fair Isle knitting:

- When changing colors, grab your new color from below. This will stop holes from forming in your work.
- Tension is key. If you make your floats (color not in use that is held at the back of your work) too tight, your hat will be puckered.
- Alternatively, if you knit too loosely, your floats may catch and pull.
- If you tend to knit tightly, it may help your tension to go up a needle size when working the Fair Isle.
- Blocking will help even out stitches.
- Chart is read right to left, and bottom to top. The pattern of the hat is a 16-stitch repeat, and each row is therefore worked 6 times per round.

HAT PATTERN

BRIM

With MC (DK and laceweight held together) and smaller needle, and using tubular CO or CO of your choice, CO 96 sts. Place marker and join in the round.
Work 1x1 ribbing until piece measures 1½" (3.75 cm) for a regular brim or 4" (10 cm) for a fold-over brim.

BODY

Work Rnds 1–40 from the chart. Break yarn, leaving a 6" (15.25 cm) tail.

FINISHING

Thread tail through remaining sts and pull to close. Weave in ends.

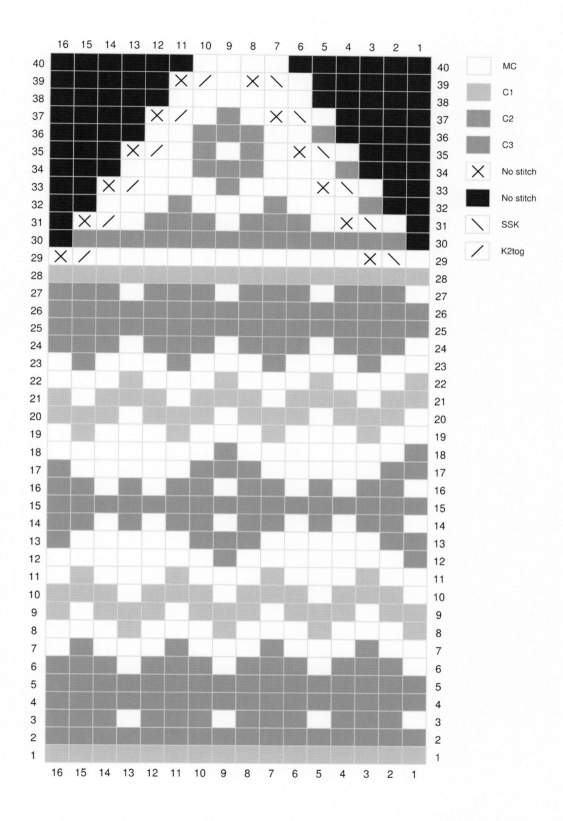

Estelle Cowl

Designed by Kunbi of Handmade by Kunbi

FINISHED MEASUREMENTS
10¼" (27.5 cm) wide and 56" (142 cm) in circumference

YARN
We Are Knitters The Petite Wool (100% wool): 3 3½ oz (100 g) skeins in Spotted Grey

HOOK
Size US J/10 (6 mm) crochet hook
Or size needed to obtain gauge

GAUGE
14 dc and 6 rows = 4" (10 cm)

SPECIAL STITCH
Shell: (3 dc, ch 2, dc) in indicated space

NOTES
- Cowl is crocheted as a flat piece and then seamed together once complete.
- You can adjust the size of the scarf (narrower or wider) by chaining a multiple of 10 stitches plus 9. To make the cowl longer, repeat Row 3 until you reach the desired length. Don't forget you will need more yarn if you would like the cowl wider or longer.

COWL PATTERN
Ch 40.

Row 1: Sc in 2nd ch from hook and in each remaining ch, turn.

Row 2: Ch 3 (counts as first dc here and throughout), dc in next st, *skip next st, shell in next st, skip 3 sts, dc in each of the next 5 sts; rep from * to last 7 sts, skip next st, shell in next st, skip 3 sts,

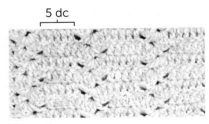

Figure 1

dc in each of the next 2 sts, turn.

Row 3: Ch 3, dc in next dc, *shell in ch-2 sp of next shell, skip next 3 dc of shell, dc in each of next 5 dc (see figure 1); rep from * across to last shell, shell in ch-2 sp of shell, dc in next dc, dc in top of turning ch, turn.

Rows 4–88: Rep Row 3.
Fasten off, leaving a long tail for seaming.

FINISHING
Lay the cowl flat. Bring the ends together and seam using preferred seaming method (mattress stitch was used for this sample). Weave in ends.

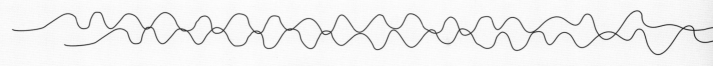

Peruvian Chill

Designed by Nathan Bryant of Loopn' Threads

FINISHED MEASUREMENTS
33¼" (84.5 cm) circumference

YARN
KnitPicks Wool of the Andes Bulky (100% Peruvian Highland wool; 137 yards [125 m] per 3½ oz [100 g] hank: 4 hanks in Mist

NEEDLES
Size US 15 (10 mm) 32" (81.5 cm) circular
Or size needed to obtain gauge

NOTIONS
Stitch marker

GAUGE
9 sts and 14 rows = 4" (10 cm) in Stockinette stitch with 2 strands held together

SPECIAL ABBREVIATION
Wrap & Turn (w&t) (see page 173)

NOTES
This cowl can be made with any bulky (weight 5) yarn of your choice. I personally would recommend the yarn I used because of the fit, drape, texture, etc. The smallest details are considered in the end result when I design handmade pieces. Think of it as a recipe: If one ingredient is changed, then the final result can be different—sometimes dramatically. I still encourage you to be creative.

COWL PATTERN

Holding 2 strands together, CO 75 sts. Being careful not to twist sts, join in the rnd and pm for beginning of rnd.

Work in St st until work measures 3" (7.5 cm) from CO edge.

W&T ROWS

Row 1: Knit to last 10 sts before marker, w&t.

Row 2 (WS): Purl to last 10 sts before marker, w&t.

Row 3 (RS): Knit to 1 st before last wrapped st, w&t.

Row 4: Purl to 1 st before last wrapped st, w&t.

Rep Rows 3 and 4 sixteen more times—18 wrapped sts on each side.

PICK UP WRAPS

Next row: Knit to wrapped st, [pick up wrap with st and knit together] 18 times, knit to marker, slip marker, k9, [pick up wrap with st and knit together] 18 times, knit to marker.

Change to working in the rnd.

Next rnd: Knit all 75 sts around.

Cont to work even in St st for 10" (25 cm).

Dec rnd: [K23, k2tog] 3 times—72 sts.

Knit 3 rnds even.

Dec rnd: [Knit 22, k2tog] 3 times—69 sts.

Knit 3 rnds even.

BO loosely.

FINISHING

The cowl has plenty of drape right off the needles, so blocking is optional.

Weave in ends.

Woodlands Sweater

Designed by Theresa Denham of Teagan and Lu

SIZE
S (M, L, XL)

FINISHED MEASUREMENTS
20 (22 ¼, 24½, 27)" [51 (57, 62, 69) cm] bust and 21 (21¾, 22½, 23¼)" [53 (55, 57, 59) cm] long

YARN
Mary Maxim Woodlands (90% acrylic, 10% alpaca; 200 yards [183 m] per 3½ oz [100 g] skein: 3 (4, 5, 6) skeins #02 Flax (Color A), 1 (1, 1, 2) skeins #08 Plum Mist (Color B), and 1 skein #13 Seafoam (Color C)

HOOK
Size US H/8 (5 mm) crochet hook

Or size needed to obtain gauge

GAUGE
14 sts and 13 rows = 4" (10 cm) in sc, dc pattern

NOTES
Sweater is designed with 3½–4" (9–10 cm) positive ease. If you want a more form-fitting version of this sweater, size down.

SWEATER PATTERN

FRONT RIBBING
With Color A, ch 11.
Row 1: Sc blo in second ch from hook and in each ch across, turn—10 sc.
Row 2: Ch 1, sc blo across, turn.

Rows 3–70 (78, 86, 94): Repeat Row 2.
Do not break yarn.

FRONT PANEL

Working into the long edge of the ribbed band:

Row 1: Ch 1, sc in each row edge across, turn—70 (78, 86, 94) sc.
Row 2: Ch 1, sc across, turn. Piece should measure approx. 20 (21¾, 23¾, 25)" [51 (55, 60, 63.5) cm] wide.
Change to Color B.
Row 3: Ch 1, hdc across, turn.
Row 4: Ch 1, hdc blo across, turn.
Row 5: Ch 1, hdc across, turn.
Row 6: Ch 1, hdc in tl across, turn.
Change to Color C.
Row 7: Ch 2 (counts as dc), cdc in next st and in each st across to last st, dc in last st.
Row 8: Ch 2 (counts as dc), dc in next st, *cdc; rep from * across to last 2 sts, dc in last 2 sts.
Change to Color B.
Row 9: Ch 1, hdc across, turn.
Row 10: Ch 1, hdc blo across, turn.
Row 11: Ch 1, hdc across, turn.
Row 12: Ch 1, hdc in tl across, turn.
Change to Color A.
Row 13: Ch 2 (counts as dc), sc in next st, *dc in next st, sc in next st; rep from * across.
Rep Row 13 until Front Panel measures 16 (17, 18, 19)" [40.5 (43, 46, 48) cm].

Shape Shoulders and Neckline

Row 1: Ch 2, sc in first st, *dc in next st, sc in next st; rep from * until you have worked 30 (34, 38, 42) sts toward center, turn, leaving remaining sts unworked.
Row 2: Ch 2, sc in first st, *dc in next st, sc in next st; rep from * to last st, dc in last st, turn.
Row 3 (dec row): Ch 2, sc in first st, *dc in next st, sc in next st; rep from * to last 3 sts, sc dec, leave last st unworked, turn—28 (32, 36, 40) sts.
Rep Rows 2–3 until 20 (22, 26, 30) sts remain, ending on Row 2. Rep for opposite shoulder by attaching yarn in the second st on the opposite outer side, and rep shoulder directions. Fasten off.
Front Panel should measure approx. 21 (21¾, 22½, 23¼)" [53 (55, 57, 59) cm] long.

BACK RIBBING

With Color A, ch 11.
Row 1: Sc blo in second ch from hook and in each ch across, turn—10 sc.
Row 2: Ch 1, sc blo across, turn.
Rows 3–70 (78, 86, 94): Rep Row 2.
Do not break yarn.

BACK PANEL

Working into the long edge of the ribbed band:
Row 1: Ch 1, sc in each row edge across, turn—70 (78, 86, 94) sc.
Row 2: Ch 1, sc across, turn.
Change to Color B.
Row 3: Ch 1, hdc across, turn.
Row 4: Ch 1, hdc blo across, turn.
Row 5: Ch 1, hdc across, turn.
Row 6: Ch 1, hdc in tl across. Turn.
Change to Color C.
Row 7: Ch 2 (counts as dc), cdc across to last st, dc in last st.
Row 8: Ch 2 (counts as dc), dc, *cdc; repeat from * across to last 2 sts, dc in last 2 sts.
Change to Color B.
Row 9: Ch 1, hdc across, turn.
Row 10: Ch 1, hdc blo across, turn.
Row 11: Ch 1, hdc across, turn.
Row 12: Ch 1, hdc in tl across, turn.
Change to Color A.
Row 13: Ch 2 (counts as dc), sc in next st, *dc in next st, sc in next st; rep from * across.
Rep Row 13 until Back Panel measures 21 (21¾, 22½, 23¼)" [53 (55, 57, 59) cm] long.
Fasten off.

SLEEVES (MAKE 2)

CUFF RIBBING

With Color A, ch 11.
Row 1: Sc blo in second ch from hook and in each ch across, turn—10 sc.
Row 2: Ch 1, sc blo across, turn.
Rep Row 2 for 38 (46, 54, 62) rows.
Do not break yarn.

SLEEVE BODY

Working into the long edge of the ribbing:

Rows 1–3: Ch 1, *dc in next st, sc in next st; repeat from * across, turn.

Row 4: (Ch 2, sc, dc) in first st, *sc in next st, dc in next st; rep from * to last st, (dc, sc, dc) in last st.

Rows 5–12: Rep Rows 1–4.

Rep Rows 3–4 two (three, four, five) times.

Fasten off.

FINISHING

ASSEMBLY

With RS facing, join shoulders of the Front and Back Panels.

Next, lay the joined piece flat, but unfolded, so both RS are facing up.

Place both Sleeves RS up and centered on each shoulder seam. Seam the Sleeves in place.

With RS facing, seam from the top of the waist ribbing up along the body and then along the Sleeve on both sides.

NECKLINE

Join yarn at the top right shoulder seam. Working into the neck edge, sc around neck twice, joining with a sl st at the end of each rnd.

Following the second rnd of sc and without breaking the yarn: Ch 3.

Row 1: Sc blo in second ch and in next ch, sl st in sc row along neck, turn.

Row 2: Ch 1, sc across, turn.

Row 3: Sc blo across, sl st in sc row along neck, turn.

Rep Rows 2 and 3 around the neck, joining with sl st at top right shoulder.

Fasten off.

Weave in all ends and lightly steam block.

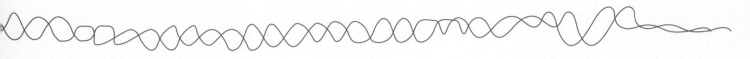

No-Sew Striped Socks

Designed by Athena Forbes of Knits N Knacks

Photography by VanLeeuwen Photography

SIZE
To fit adult Medium

FINISHED MEASUREMENTS
6¾" (17 cm) in circumference

YARN
Allison Barnes Basic Sock (80% superwash Merino, 20% nylon; 420 yards [385 m] per 4 oz [115 g] hank): 1 hank each You Had Me at Merlot (MC) and Whomp There It Is (discontinued) (CC) Scrap yarn for provisional cast-on

NEEDLES
Size US 1 (2.25 mm) double-pointed needles or 32" (81 cm) circular for magic loop
Or size needed to obtain gauge

GAUGE
38 sts and 50 rows = 4" (10 cm) in Stockinette stitch, unblocked

SPECIAL STITCHES
Wrap
w&t (wrap and turn)
Working Stitches with Wraps

NOTES
- The pattern is written to be worked toe-up with a short-row toe and heel; it can, however, be worked top-down just as easily. You can also substitute your toe and heel of choice.
- If you already knit your socks so they are very snug on your feet, I recommend adding 2–4 stitches to the total stitch count, as the spiral will snug the sock up slightly.
- ToNote that "wrap" here is a special stitch that is not the same as a wrap within w&t (wrap and turn).
- keep cutting your yarn to a minimum, the heel will be worked in the same color of the stripe that it falls in.
- I used the Mimi Codd short-row heel/toe method.
- To keep holes in the short-row toe and heel to a minimum, knit/purl the stitch after your wrap tighter than usual.
- If you knit Continental style, you can work the sock without ever dropping the working color by using your right hand to work the spiral.

SOCK PATTERN

SHORT-ROW TOE

With scrap yarn, provisionally CO 32 sts (see page 166).

With MC:

*Row 1 (RS): K to last st, w&t.

Row 2 (WS): P to last st, w&t.

Row 3: K to 1 st before next wrapped st, w&t.

Row 4: P to 1 st before next wrapped st, w&t.

Rep Rows 3 and 4 until you have 10 (10, 12, 12, 12, 14, 14) unwrapped sts in the center of your short-row sections.

Row 5: K to first wrapped st, k the st and its wrap together tbl, w&t.

Row 6: P to first wrapped st, p the st and its wrap together, w&t.

Row 7: K to double-wrapped st, k the st and its wraps together tbl, w&t.

Row 8: P to first double-wrapped st, p the st and its wraps together, w&t.

Repeat Rows 7 and 8 until all wraps have been knitted together with their sts.**

Remove provisional CO, inserting your unused needles into the sts. You should now have 64 sts on your needles and will begin working in the rnd.

Knit 1 rnd in MC.

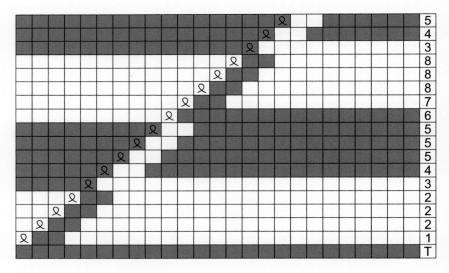

The T on the chart represents the toe, and the numbers up the side correspond with the round numbers. MC is gray and CC is white. The loop symbol represents a wrap. The chart is read from bottom to top; each row is read from right to left.

FOOT

STRIPE 1

Rnd 1: With CC, k to last 3 MC sts, pick up MC from *under* CC (twisting the 2 strands around each other), k2 in MC, drop MC, pick up CC (undoing the previous twist), k1 in CC, wrap.

Note: The beginning of the rnd, which starts after the wrapped st, will move forward 1 st each rnd so that it is always after the previous wrap.

Rnd 2: K around in CC until 1 CC st remains, drop CC, pick up MC from *under* CC, k2 with MC, drop MC (as in Rnd 1), pick up CC, k1 with CC, wrap.

Rep Rnd 2 six times, or for desired number of rnds for longer or shorter stripes.

STRIPE 2

Rnd 3: (changing from CC to MC) K with CC until only 1 st of MC remains, drop CC, pick up MC (without twisting strands), k1 in MC, wrap.

Rnd 4: K around in MC until 3 sts of CC remain, drop MC, pick up CC from *under* MC, k2 in CC, drop CC, pick up MC (without twisting strands), k1, wrap.

Rnd 5: K around in MC until 1 MC st remains before a CC st, drop MC, pick up CC from *under* MC, k2 in CC, drop CC, pick up MC (without twisting strands), k1, wrap.

Rep Rnd 5 six times, or for desired number of rnds.

STRIPE 3

Rnd 6: (changing from MC to CC) K in MC until 1 st of CC twist remains, drop MC, pick up CC (without twisting strands), k1 in CC, wrap.

Rnd 7: K around in CC until 3 sts of MC remain, drop CC, pick up MC from *under* CC, k2 in MC, drop MC, pick up CC (without twisting strands), k1, wrap.

Rnd 8: K around in CC until 1 CC st remains before a MC st, drop CC, pick up MC from *under* CC, k2 in MC, drop MC, pick up CC (without twisting strands), k1, wrap.

Repeat Rnd 8 six times, or for desired number of rnds.

Repeat Rnds 3–8 until Foot is 1¾" (4.5 cm) shorter than the desired total length needed.

HEEL

Repeat the instructions for the Short-Row Toe from * to **, beginning Heel on the opposite side of the sock from the spiral (do not work the heel over the spiral).

LEG

Continue in pattern as established until desired length, ending after Rnd 3.
Knit 1 rnd in MC.

CUFF

Rnd 1: With MC, *K1, p1; rep from * to end of rnd.
Repeat Rnd 1 until Cuff measures 2" (5 cm).
BO using a tubular BO or BO of your choice.

FINISHING

Weave in ends.

Glamjamas

Designed by Kate Hammitt of
One of A Kate

SIZE

Pants: S/M (L/XL)
Top: XS (S, M, L, XL)
*Sample is shown in size S/M
pants and S top.*

FINISHED MEASUREMENTS

Pants:
Band circumference 34" (42")
[86.5 (106.5) cm]
Length 36" (38") [91.5 (96.5) cm]
Top:
Bust circumference 30" (34", 38",
42", 46") [76 (86.5, 96.5, 106.5,
117) cm]
Length 16½" (17", 17¼", 17.5",
17¾") [42 (43, 44, 44.5, 45) cm]
Arm depth 6½" (7", 7½", 8", 8½")
[16.5 (18, 19, 20.5, 21.5) cm]
Sleeve length, all sizes: 18"
[45.5 cm]

YARN

Berroco Modern Cotton DK
(60% pima cotton, 40% modal
rayon; 335 yards [306 m] per 3½
oz [100 g] hank): 7 (8) hanks in
#6601 Sandy Point (Color A) and
3 (4) hanks in #6618 Coffee Milk
(Color B)

HOOK

US size B/1 (2.25 mm) crochet
hook

NEEDLES

US size 5 (3.75 mm) 40"
(101.5 cm) circular needle

NOTIONS

Stitch markers
Stitch holder or scrap yarn
(optional)
Optional: no-fray glue, metal/
clear aglets, or beads

GAUGE

19 sts and 12 rows = 4" (10 cm)
in BLdc
17 sts and 37 rounds = 4" (10 cm)
in Stockinette stitch

SPECIAL STITCHES

Picot: Ch 3, sl st in first ch.
Third Loop: behind front and
back loops

NOTES

- The Glamjamas were designed
  as a set that can be worn
  separately as nightwear or
  everyday wear.
- With the recommended
  Berroco Modern Cotton,
  you are sure to be lounging
  in luxury. Keep in mind that
  cotton is known to stretch
  with wear.
- Using both crochet and
  knitting techniques, this set

is constructed from the top down for the pants and from the bottom up for the shirt. The body of the shirt is the only knitted section.

- Beginning chains do NOT count as stitches.

PAJAMA PANTS

I-CORD

With color A and crochet hook:

Row 1: Ch 3, draw up 1 loop from each of first 2 ch, carefully remove 2 loops from hook, yo, pull through loop on hook, *insert hook into next dropped loop, yo, pull through; rep from * once more.

Rep Row 1 until you reach desired hip circumference plus 24" (61 cm). *(Sample measures 64" [162.5 cm].)* Cut yarn and pull through all loops on hook to fasten off. Optional: Adorn ends with metal aglets, beads, clear shoelace tips, or no-fray glue. *(Sample used no-fray glue to achieve a shoelace-tip look.)*

BAND

With color A and crochet hook:

Row 1: Fsc 30.

Row 2: Ch 1, turn, sc blo across.

Rep Row 2 for a total of 144 (176) rows. Do not fasten off.

ASSEMBLE BAND

Fold band lengthwise. Lay i-cord inside band. Bring folded short ends together to form tube. Joining four layers of short ends together, sl st 20, sl st through folded end on one side of next 5 sts (this will create an opening where the i-cord will feed through), sl st to join next 5 sts of both ends. Do not fasten off. Ch1, sc 210 (252) evenly across the bottom, enclosing i-cord in band; sl st to first sc. Do not fasten off; continue to legs.

LEGS

Legs are constructed in vertical rows, joining to the band as you work:

Row 1: Yo, insert hook in next st, yo, pull up a loop, yo, pull through 1 loop, (yo, pull through 2 loops) twice; continue to Fdc for 34 (38) sts.

Row 2: Ch 1, turn, dc in first st, FLdc across, sl st in next 3 sts on band.

Row 3: Turn, BLdc 33 (37), dc in both loops of last st, Fdc 116 (122).

Row 4: Ch 1, turn, dc in first st, FLdc in next 149 (159) sts, sl st in next 3 sts.

Row 5: Turn, BLdc in next 149 (159) sts, dc through both loops of last st.

Rep Rows 4 and 5 until you reach a total of 67 (71) long rows.

Next row: Turn, BLdc in next 37 (41) sts, dc through both loops of next st.

To customize: Measure from the same position between your legs from above to back waist. This should be the length of the band plus the short rows opposite the icord-opening side. Add more stitches if needed.

Next row: Ch 1, turn, dc in first st, FLdc in next 37 (41) sts, sl st in next 3 sts.

Rep the previous 2 rows twice.

Rep Row 3.

Rep Rows 4 and 5 until you reach a total of 66 (80) long rows.

Fasten off, leaving a tail 3 times the length of short row.

FINISHING

With WS facing, use long tail to mattress stitch the beginning short row to 34 (38) sts of last long row. For ideal seamless look, stitch through both loops on one side and front loop on opposite side.

With WS facing, attach yarn 3 times the length of both legs to bottom of one leg. Seamlessly mattress stitch, starting with first leg, using same method as above until you reach the short rows. Whip st the front short rows to

the back short rows. Continue to seamlessly mattress stitch the second leg. Fasten off. Weave in ends.

PAJAMA TOP

BAND

With color A and crochet hook:
Row 1: Fsc 15 sts.
Row 2: Ch 1, turn, sc in first st, BLsc in next 13 sts, sc in both loops of last st.
Rep Row 2 for a total of 146 (164, 182, 200, 218) rows.

Sl st across 15 sts on both ends to join. Fasten off.

BODY

Flip band inside out, so RS is facing and seam is hidden on WS. With color A and circular knitting needles:
Pick up 146 (164, 182, 200, 218) sts, pm for beginning of rnd.
Knit around for 133 (138, 140, 142, 145) rows or until desired length.
Split for sleeves:

*__Row 1:__ With Color B, k73 (82, 91, 100, 109), turn.
Hold remaining sts on cord or place on st holder or scrap yarn.
Row 2: P73 (82, 91, 100, 109), turn.
Rep Rows 1 and 2 for a total of 60 (65, 70, 75, 80) rows.
Next row: K13 (15, 17, 19, 21), BO 47 (52, 57, 62, 67), k13 (15, 17, 19, 21).
Place live sts on st holder or scrap yarn. Transfer held sts to needle.

Rep from * with first set of sts placed on hold.

With WS facing, use three-needle BO to seam front and back shoulders together.

SLEEVES (MAKE 2)

With color B and crochet hook, and with RS facing, attach yarn to center of underarm:

Rnd 1: Working into knit ends, ch 2, sc 119 (129, 139, 149, 159), sl st to first sc to join.

For the remainder of the pattern, crochet into the third loop.

Rnd 2: Ch 2, dc2tog, dc 115 (125, 135, 145, 155), dc2tog, sl st to first dc to join—117 (127, 137, 147, 157) sts.

Rnd 3: Ch 2, dc2tog, dc 55 (60, 65, 70, 75), FPdc, dc, FPdc, dc 55 (60, 65, 70, 75), dc2tog, sl st to first dc to join—115 (125, 135, 145, 155) sts.

Rnd 4: Ch 2, dc2tog, dc 54 (59, 64, 69, 74), FPdc, dc, FPdc, dc 54 (59, 64, 69, 74), dc2tog, sl st to first dc to join—113 (123, 133, 143, 153) sts.

Rnd 5: Ch 2, dc2tog, dc 53 (58, 63, 68, 73), FPdc, dc, FPdc, dc 53 (58, 63, 68, 73), dc2tog, sl st to first dc to join—111 (121, 131, 141, 151) sts.

Rnd 6: Ch 2, dc2tog, dc 52 (57, 62, 67, 72), sk 2, FPTr around FPdc, dc in last sk st behind FPTr just made, FPTr around first sk FPdc in front of first FPTr, dc 52 (57, 62, 67, 72), dc2tog, sl st to first dc to join —109 (119, 129, 139, 149) sts.

Rnd 7: Ch 2, dc2tog, dc 51 (56, 61, 66, 71), FPdc around FPTr, dc, FPdc around FPTr, dc 51 (56, 61, 66, 71), dc2tog, sl st to first dc to join—107 (117, 127, 137, 147) sts.

Rnd 8: Ch 2, dc2tog, dc 50 (55, 60, 65, 70, FPdc, dc, FPdc, dc 50 (55, 60, 65, 70), dc2tog, sl st to first dc to join—105 (115, 125, 135, 145) sts.

Rnd 9: Ch 2, dc2tog, dc 49 (54, 59, 64, 69), FPdc, dc, FPdc, dc 49 (54, 59, 64, 69), dc2tog, sl st to first dc to join—103 (113, 123, 133, 143) sts.

Rnd 10: Ch 2, dc2tog, dc 48 (53, 58, 63, 68), sk 2, FPTr around FPdc, dc in last sk st behind FPTr just made, FPTr around first sk FPdc in front of first FPTr, dc 48 (53, 58, 63, 68), dc2tog, sl st to first dc to join—101 (111, 121, 131, 141) sts.

Rnd 11: Ch 2, dc 47 (52, 57, 62, 67), FPdc around FPTr, dc, FPdc around FPTr, dc 47 (52, 57, 62, 67), sl st to first dc to join—99 (109, 119, 129, 139) sts.

Rnd 12: Ch 2, dc 46 (51, 56, 61, 66), FPdc, dc, FPdc, dc 46 (51, 56, 61, 66), sl st to first dc to join—97 (107, 117, 127, 137) sts.

Rnd 13: Ch 2, dc2tog, dc 45 (50, 55, 60, 65), FPdc, dc, FPdc, dc 45 (50, 55, 60, 65), dc2tog, sl st to first dc to join—95 (105, 115, 125, 135) sts.

Rnd 14: Ch 2, dc2tog, dc 44 (49, 54, 59, 64), sk 2, FPTr around FPdc, dc in last sk st behind FPTr just made, FPTr around first sk FPdc in front of first FPTr, dc 44 (49, 54, 59, 64), dc2tog, sl st to first dc to join—93 (103, 113, 123, 133) sts.

Rnd 15: Ch 2, dc2tog, dc 43 (48, 53, 58, 63), FPdc around FPTr, dc, FPdc around FPTr, dc 43 (48, 53, 58, 63), dc2tog, sl st to first dc to join—91 (101, 111, 121, 131) sts.

Rnd 16: Ch 2, dc2tog, dc 42 (47, 52, 57, 62), FPdc, dc, FPdc, dc 42 (47, 52, 57, 62), dc2tog, sl st to first dc to join—89 (99, 109, 119, 129) sts.

Rnd 17: Ch 2, dc2tog, dc 41 (46, 51, 56, 61), FPdc, dc, FPdc, dc 41 (46, 51, 56, 61), dc2tog, sl st to first dc to join—87 (97, 107, 117, 127) sts.

Rnd 18: Ch 2, dc2tog, dc 40 (45, 50, 55, 60), sk 2, FPTr around FPdc, dc in last sk st behind FPTr just made, FPTr around first sk FPdc in front of first FPTr, dc 40 (45, 50, 55, 60), dc2tog, sl st to first dc to join—85 (95, 105, 115, 125) sts.

Rnd 19: Ch 2, dc2tog, dc 39 (44, 49, 54, 59), FPdc around FPTr, dc, FPdc around FPTr, dc 39 (44, 49, 54, 59), dc2tog, sl st to first dc to join—83 (93, 103, 113, 123) sts.

Rnd 20: Ch 2, dc2tog, dc 38 (43, 48, 53, 58), FPdc, dc, FPdc, dc 38 (43, 48, 53, 58), dc2tog, sl st to first dc to join—81 (91, 101, 111, 121) sts.

Rnd 21: Ch 2, dc2tog, dc 37 (42, 47, 52, 57), FPdc, dc, FPdc, dc 37 (42, 47, 52, 57), dc2tog, sl st to first dc to join—79 (89, 99, 109, 119) sts.

Rnd 22: Ch 2, dc2tog, dc 36 (41, 46, 51, 56), sk 2, FPTr around FPdc, dc in last sk st behind FPTr just made, FPTr around first sk FPdc in front of first FPTr, dc 36 (41, 46, 51, 56), dc2tog, sl st to first dc to join—77 (87, 97, 107, 117) sts.

Rnd 23: Ch 2, dc2tog, dc 35 (40, 45, 50, 55), FPdc around FPTr, dc, FPdc around FPTr, dc 35 (40, 45, 50, 55), dc2tog, sl st to first dc to join—75 (85, 95, 105, 115) sts.

Rnd 24: Ch 2, dc2tog, dc 34 (39, 44, 49, 54), FPdc, dc, FPdc, dc 34 (39, 44, 49, 54), dc2tog, sl st to first dc to join—73 (83, 93, 103, 113) sts.

Rnd 25: Ch 2, dc2tog, dc 33 (38, 43, 48, 53), FPdc, dc, FPdc, dc 33 (38, 43, 48, 53), dc2tog, sl st to first dc to join—71 (81, 91, 101, 111) sts.

Rnd 26: Ch 2, dc2tog, dc 32 (37, 42, 47, 52), sk 2, FPTr around FPdc, dc in last sk st behind FPTr just made, FPTr around first sk FPdc in front of first FPTr, dc 32 (37, 42, 47, 52), dc2tog, sl st to first dc to join—69 (79, 89, 99, 109) sts.

Rnd 27: Ch 2, dc2tog, dc 31 (36, 41, 46, 51), FPdc around FPTr, dc, FPdc around FPTr, dc 31 (36, 41, 46, 51), dc2tog, sl st to first dc to join—67 (77, 87, 97, 107) sts.

Rnd 28: Ch 2, dc2tog, dc 30 (35, 40, 45, 50), FPdc, dc, FPdc, dc 30 (35, 40, 45, 50), dc2tog, sl st to first dc to join—65 (75, 85, 95, 105) sts.

Rnd 29: Ch 2, dc2tog, dc 29 (34, 39, 44, 49), FPdc, dc, FPdc, dc 29 (34, 39, 44, 49), dc2tog, sl st to first dc to join—63 (73, 83, 93, 103) sts.

Rnd 30: Ch 2, dc2tog, dc 28 (33, 38, 43, 48), sk 2, FPTr around FPdc, dc in last sk st behind FPTr just made, FPTr around first sk FPdc in front of first FPTr, dc 28 (33, 38, 43, 48), dc2tog, sl st to first dc to join—61 (71, 81, 91, 101) sts.

Rnd 31: Ch 2, dc2tog, dc 27 (32, 37, 42, 47), FPdc around FPTr, dc, FPdc around FPTr, dc 27 (32, 37, 42, 47), dc2tog, sl st to first dc to join—59 (69, 79, 89, 99) sts.

Rnd 32: Ch 2, dc2tog, dc 26 (31, 36, 41, 46), FPdc, dc, FPdc, dc 26 (31, 36, 41, 46), dc2tog, sl st to first dc to join—57 (67, 77, 87, 97) sts.

Rnd 33: Ch 2, dc2tog, dc 25 (30, 35, 40, 45), FPdc, dc, FPdc, dc 25 (30, 35, 40, 45), dc2tog, sl st to first dc to join—55 (65, 75, 85, 95) sts.

Rnd 34: Ch 2, dc2tog, dc 24 (29, 34, 39, 44), sk 2, FPTr around FPdc, dc in last sk st behind FPTr just made, FPTr around first sk FPdc in front of first FPTr, dc 24 (29, 34, 39, 44), dc2tog, sl st to first dc to join—53 (63, 73, 83, 93) st.

Rnd 35: Ch 2, dc 25 (30, 35, 40, 45), FPdc around FPTr, dc, FPdc around FPTr, dc 25 (30, 35, 40, 45), sl st to first dc to join—53 (63, 73, 83, 93) sts.

Rnd 36: Ch 2, dc 25 (30, 35, 40, 45), FPdc, dc, FPdc, dc 25 (30, 35, 40, 45), sl st to first dc to join—53 (63, 73, 83, 93) sts.

Rnd 37: Rep Rnd 36.

Rnd 38: Ch 2, dc 25 (30, 35, 40, 45), sk 2, FPTr around FPdc, dc in last sk st behind FPTr just made, FPTr around first sk FPdc in front of first FPTr, dc 25 (30, 35, 40, 45), sl st to first dc to join—53 (63, 73, 83, 93) sts.

Rep Rnds 35–38 until you have worked a total of 65 rows or until desired length.

Fasten off.

FINISHING

Weave in ends.

Scandinavian Summer Dress

Designed by Ulrikke Henninen of High in Fiber

Photography by Edward Daniel

SIZE
XS (S, M, L, XL)

FINISHED MEASUREMENTS
To fit 28–30 (32–34, 36–38, 40–42, 44–46)" [71–76 (81–86, 91–96, 101–106, 112–117) cm] bust

YARN
Lana Gatto Nuovo Jaipur (100% Egyptian mako cotton; 110 yards [100 m] per 1¾ oz [50 g] skein): 12 (14, 16, 18, 20) skeins in #6565 Snow

HOOK
Size US E/4 (3.5 mm) crochet hook
Or size needed to obtain gauge

NOTES
- This dress is designed to be pulled over your head when putting it on.
- The bodice is made with a mesh stitch and will have some elasticity to it. Keep this in mind when choosing your preferred size; the measuring tape will feel a little tighter around your chest than the finished product.
- The skirt is attached directly to the bodice and will therefore need no individual stitch count information.
- Even when using a similar-weight and -length yarn substitute, the amount of yarn needed will vary depending on the cotton qualities, such as pima or mercerized. These minor differences in texture can influence the amount of yarn needed.

GAUGE
18 sts and 10 rows = 4" (10 cm)
in dc

DRESS PATTERN

FRONT BODICE

Ch 72 (76, 80, 88, 92).

Row 1: Sc in 2nd ch from hook
and in each ch across, turn—71
(75, 79, 87, 91) sc.

Row 2: Ch 4 (counts as dc + ch 1
here and throughout), skip 1 st,
*dc in next st, ch 1, skip ch-1 sp;
rep from * to last st, dc in last st,
turn.

Rows 3–20: Ch 4, skip ch-1 sp,
*dc in next st, ch 1, skip ch-1 sp;
rep from * to last st, dc in 3rd ch
of turning ch, turn.

Row 21: Ch 4, [skip ch-1 sp, dc
in next st, ch 1] 16 (17, 18, 20, 21)
times, dc in next st, dc in ch-1 sp,
dc in next st, *ch 1, skip ch-1 sp,
dc in next st; rep from * to end of
row, turn.

Row 22: Ch 4, *skip ch-1 sp, dc
in next st, ch 1; rep from * to last
dc before center dc block, (dc in
st, dc in ch-1 sp) 3 times, dc in
next st, **ch 1, skip ch-1 sp, dc
in next st; rep from ** to end of
row, turn.

Rows 23–34: Rep Row 22,
increasing center dc block by
adding 2 dc sts on each side of

the block—55 center dc sts after Row 34.

Row 35: Ch 1, sc in each st and ch-1 sp across.

Fasten off, leaving a long strand for shoulder seam.

BODICE BACK

Ch 72 (76, 80, 88, 92).

Row 1: Sc 2nd ch from hook and in each ch across—71 (75, 79, 87, 91) sc.

Row 2: Ch 4 (counts as dc + ch 1 here and throughout), skip 1 st, *dc in next st, ch 1, skip 1 st; rep from * to last st, dc in last st, turn.

Rows 3–33: Ch 4, skip ch-1 sp, *dc in next st, ch 1, skip ch-1 sp; rep from * to last st, dc in 3rd ch of turning ch, turn.

Row 34: Ch 4, skip ch-1 sp, *dc in next st, ch 1, skip ch-1 sp; rep from * to last st, dc in last st, turn.

Row 35: Ch 1, sc in each st and ch-1 sp across.

Fasten off, leaving a long strand for shoulder seam.

SHOULDER SEAMS

Place Bodice Front and Back with RS together. Using the long strands you left after Row 35, seam from one edge toward the center through the sc in Row 35 of each piece. The number of sts seamed depends on the

preferred neckline width; the example in the photo is size XS, and the first 9 sts on each side have been seamed.

Repeat on the opposite edge of the neckline, seaming from the edge toward the center.

SIDE SEAMS

With RS together and starting at the bottom edge, seam the sides. The example in the photo has a seam from Rows 1–18, but choose your seam length based on preferred armhole depth. Turn completed Bodice right side out.

SKIRT

With Bodice Back facing, insert hook into a foundation ch near the left edge (which will be the front when wearing the dress).

Rnd 1: Ch 1, sc in each foundation ch around; sl st in first sc to join—142 (150, 158, 174, 182) sc.

Rnd 2: Ch 3 (counts as dc here and throughout), dc in each st around; sl st in 3rd ch to join.

Rnd 3: Ch 3, 2 dc in each st around, dc until you reach the ch 3 from the beginning of the round. Place 1 dc in the same st as the ch 3 (to make sure you have 2 dc also in this st); sl st in 3rd ch to join—284 (300, 316, 348, 364) dc.

Rnds 4–32: Ch 3, dc in each st around; sl st in 3rd ch to join. Note: If you want to make the skirt longer, add extra rows of dc after Rnd 32. The remaining section (Rnds 33–44) measures approx. 4¾" (12 cm).

Rnd 33: Ch 4 (counts as 1 dc + ch 1), *skip 1 st, dc in next st, ch 1; rep from * to end of rnd; sl st in 3rd ch to join.

Rnd 34: Ch 3, dc in each st around; sl st in 3rd ch to join.

Rnds 35–36: Rep Rnd 33.

Rnd 37: Rep Rnd 34.

Rnds 38–43: Rep Rnd 33.

Rnd 44: Ch 1, sc in each st around; sl st in first sc to join.

Fasten off.

FINISHING

CORD

Create a foundation ch long enough to fit around your waist, plus extra length for tying it. The cord will be tied together on the *inside* of the dress.

Starting with the cord placed inside the dress, feed the Cord through Row 2 of the Front and Back Bodice as follows: *under* one dc, *over* the next dc. Finish with the cord placed *inside* the dress.

Weave in ends.

The Traveler Hoodie

Designed by Rachel Misner of Evelyn and Peter

SIZE
XS (S, M, L, XL, 2X, 3X, 4X)

FINISHED MEASUREMENTS
18 (19, 20, 21, 22, 23, 24, 25)" [46 (28, 51, 53, 56, 58, 61, 63.5) cm] long (shoulder to hem)
20¾ (22, 23¼, 24½, 25¾, 27, 28¼, 29½)" [53 (56, 59, 62, 65.5, 69, 72, 75) cm] wide
20 (20¼, 20½, 20¾, 21, 21¼, 21½, 21¾)" [51 (51.5, 52, 53, 53, 54, 54.5, 55) cm] sleeve length (armpit to cuff)

YARN
Lion Brand Jeans (100% acrylic; 246 yards [225 m] per 3½ oz [100 g] skein): 5 (6, 6, 6, 7, 7, 7, 7) skeins #150 Vintage

HOOK
Size US H/8 (5 mm) crochet hook
Or size needed to obtain gauge

NOTE
The body and hood are worked in three separate panels before joining. The sleeves are added last and worked in the round.

GAUGE
13 sts and 12 rows = 4" (10 cm) in esc

HOODIE PATTERN

BACK PANEL
Ch 9.

Row 1: Sc blo in 2nd ch from hook and in each ch across, turn—8 sc.

Rows 2–68 (72, 76, 80, 84, 88, 92, 96): Ch 1, sc blo in each st across, turn.

Working along the top of the ribbing, create the body:

Row 1: Ch 1, work 1 esc into the end of each row across ribbing, turn—68 (72, 76, 80, 84, 88, 92, 96) esc.

Rows 2–34 (36, 38, 40, 42, 44, 46, 48): Ch 1, esc in each st across, turn.

ARMHOLE SHAPING
Row 35 (37, 39, 41, 43, 45, 47, 49): Sl st in first 8 (8, 9, 9, 10, 10, 11, 11) sts, esc in each st across to last 8 (8, 9, 9, 10, 10, 11, 11) sts, turn, leaving last sts unworked—52 (56, 58, 62, 64, 68, 70, 74) Esc.

Rows 36 (38, 40, 42, 44, 46, 48, 50)–45 (48, 51, 54, 57, 60, 63, 66): Ch 1, esc in each st across, turn.

Rows 46 (49, 52, 55, 58, 61, 64, 67)–48 (51, 54, 57, 60, 63, 66, 69): Ch 1, esc in next 22 (24, 25, 27, 28, 30, 31, 33) sts, turn—22 (24, 25, 27, 28, 30, 31, 33) esc.
Fasten off.

With RS facing and preparing to work RS row, count 22 (24, 25, 27, 28, 30, 31, 33) sts in toward center of panel on opposite side. Join yarn with a sl st.
Rep Rows 46 (49, 52, 55, 58, 61, 64, 67)–48 (51, 54, 57, 60, 63, 66, 69) on opposite side to create second shoulder.
Fasten off.

FRONT PANEL (MAKE 2)
Ch 9.

Row 1: 1 Sc blo in 2nd ch from hook and in each ch across, turn—8 sc.

Rows 2–34 (36, 38, 40, 42, 44, 46, 48): Ch 1, sc blo in each st across, turn.

Working along the top of the ribbing to create the body:

Row 1: Ch 1, work 1 esc into the end of each row across ribbing, turn—34 (36, 38, 40, 42, 44, 46, 48) esc.

Rows 2–34 (36, 38, 40, 42, 44, 46, 48): Ch 1, esc in each st across, turn.

ARMHOLE SHAPING
Row 35 (37, 39, 41, 43, 45, 47, 49): Sl st in first 8 (8, 9, 9, 10, 10, 11, 11) sts, esc in each remaining st across, turn—26 (28, 29, 31, 32, 34, 35, 37) esc.

Rows 36 (38, 40, 42, 44, 46, 48, 50)–39 (41, 43, 45, 47, 49, 51, 53): Ch 1, esc in each st across, turn.

NECKLINE SHAPING
Row 40 (42, 44, 46, 48, 50, 52, 54): Ch 1, esc2tog, esc in each st across, turn—25 (27, 28, 30, 31, 33, 34, 36) esc.

Row 41 (43, 45, 47, 49, 51, 53, 55): Ch 1, 1 esc in each st to last 2 sts, esc2tog—24 (26, 27, 29, 30, 32, 33, 35) esc.

Row 42 (44, 46, 48, 50, 52, 54, 56): Rep Row 40—23 (25, 26, 28, 29, 31, 32, 34) esc.

Row 43 (45, 47, 49, 51, 53, 55, 57): Rep Row 41—22 (24, 25, 27, 28, 30, 31, 33) esc.

Rows 44 (46, 48, 50, 52, 54, 56, 58)–48 (51, 54, 57, 60, 63, 66, 69): Ch 1, esc in each st across, turn.
Fasten off.

JOIN FRONTS TO BACK
Lay Front Panels on top of Back Panel with WS facing. Using slip st or mattress st, seam both Front Panels to the Back Panel at the shoulders. Then seam both sides together from the bottom ribbing edge up to the armhole shaping row.

SLEEVES (MAKE 2)
Note: Sleeves are worked in joined rnds. Each rnd is joined with a sl st before turning.
With RS facing, join yarn to the bottom armhole seam with a sl st.

Rnd 1: Ch 1, work 42 (44, 48, 50, 54, 56, 60, 62) esc evenly around armhole; join to first st with a sl st, turn.

Rnds 2–18: Ch 1, esc in each st around; join to first st with a slip st, turn.

Rnd 19: Ch 1, esc in first 19 (20, 22, 23, 25, 26, 28, 29) sts, esc2tog, esc in next 19 (20, 22, 23, 25, 26, 28, 29) sts, esc2tog; join to first st with a slip st, turn—40 (42, 46, 48, 52, 54, 58, 60) esc.

Rnds 20–24: Ch 1, Esc in each st around; join to first st with a slip st, turn.

Rnd 25: Ch 1, esc in first 18 (19, 21, 22, 24, 25, 27, 28) sts, esc2tog, esc in next 18 (19, 21, 22, 24, 25, 27, 28) sts, esc2tog; join to first st with a slip st, turn—38 (40, 44, 46, 50, 52, 56, 58) esc.

Rnds 26–29: Ch 1, esc in each st around; join to first st with a slip st, turn.

Rnd 30: Ch 1, esc in first 17 (18, 20, 21, 23, 24, 26, 27) sts, esc2tog, esc in next 17 (18, 20, 21, 23, 24, 26, 27) sts, esc2tog; join to first st with a slip st, turn—36 (38, 42, 44, 48, 50, 54, 56) esc.

Rnds 31–33: Ch 1, esc in each st around; join to first st with a slip st, turn.

Rnd 34: Ch 1, esc in first 16 (17, 19, 20, 22, 23, 25, 26) sts, esc2tog, esc in next 16 (17, 19, 20, 22, 23, 25, 26) sts, esc2tog; join to first st with a slip st, turn—34 (36, 40, 42, 46, 48, 52, 54) esc.

Rnds 35–36: Ch 1, esc in each st around; join to first st with a slip st, turn.

Rnd 37: Ch 1, esc in first 15 (16, 18, 19, 21, 22, 24, 25) sts, esc2tog, esc in next 15 (16, 18, 19, 21, 22, 24, 25) esc, esc2tog; join to first st with a slip st, turn—32 (34, 38, 40, 44, 46, 50, 52) esc.

Rnds 38–52 (53, 53, 53, 54, 54, 54, 54): Ch 1, esc in each st around; join to first st with a slip st, turn. Note: If you would like your sleeve to be less baggy, cont to add 2 dec every 3rd rnd in Rnds 38–52 (53, 53, 53, 54, 54, 54, 54) until you reach the desired circumference.

Try on the sweater to determine if you need more or less length in the sleeve. Adjust accordingly before moving to the cuff. Note: The cuff will add about 1" (2.5 cm) of length.

CUFF

Rnds 53 (54, 54, 54, 55, 55, 55, 55)–56 (57, 57, 57, 58, 58, 58, 58): Ch 2 (counts as dc), *bpdc in next st, fpdc in next st; rep from * around; join to top of ch 2 with a sl st, do not turn—32 (34, 38, 40, 44, 46, 50, 52) dc.
Fasten off.

HOOD

With RS facing, join yarn to the front left panel at Row 40 (42, 44, 46, 48, 50, 52, 54) (where neckline shaping began) with a sl st.

Row 1: Ch 1, work esc evenly up the side of the front panel, across the back neckline, and down the second front panel (until you reach neckline shaping edge) for a total of 34 (36, 38, 40, 42, 44, 46, 48) esc, turn.

Rows 2 and 3: Ch 1, esc in each st across, turn.

Row 4: Ch 1, esc in first 8 (9, 10, 11, 12, 13, 14, 15) sts, 2 esc in next st, esc in next 16 sts, 2 esc in next st, esc in next 8 (9, 10, 11, 12, 13, 14, 15) sts, turn—36 (38, 40, 42, 44, 46, 48, 50) esc.

Row 5: Ch 1, esc in each st across, turn.

Row 6: Ch 1, *esc in next 5 sts, 2 esc in next st; rep from * across row to last 0 (2, 4, 0, 2, 4, 0, 2) sts, esc in last 0 (2, 4, 0, 2, 4, 0, 2) sts, turn—42 (44, 46, 49, 51, 53, 56, 58) esc.

Row 7: Rep Row 5.

Row 8: Ch 1, *2 esc in next st, esc in next 6 sts; repeat from * across row to last 0 (2, 4, 0, 2, 4, 0, 2) sts, esc in last 0 (2, 4, 0, 2, 4, 0, 2) sts, turn—48 (50, 52, 56, 58, 60, 64, 66) esc.

Row 9: Rep Row 5.

Row 10: Ch 1, *esc in next 7 sts, 2 esc in next st; repeat from * across row to last 0 (2, 4, 0, 2, 4, 0, 2) sts, esc in last 0 (2, 4, 0, 2, 4, 0, 2) sts, turn—54 (56, 58, 63, 65, 67, 72, 74 Esc.

Rows 11 and 12: Rep Row 5.

Row 13: Ch 1, *2 esc in next st, esc in next 8 sts; rep from * across row to last 0 (2, 4, 0, 2, 4, 0, 2) sts, esc in last 0 (2, 4, 0, 2, 4, 0, 2) sts, turn—60 (62, 64, 70, 72, 74, 80, 82) esc.

Rows 14–32: Rep Row 5.
Turn Hood RS out. Insert hook in the outer loops only of your first and last st of Row 32 and make a sl st. Cont across the row until the entire row is seamed.
Fasten off.

FINISHING

TRIM

With sweater RS out, join yarn with a sl st to the bottom left corner of the Front Panel.

Row 1: Ch 2 (counts as dc), work 1 dc into end of each row up the side of the first Front Panel; work 1 dc in the end of each row up the first side of the Hood and down the opposite side; work 1 dc down the side of the second Front Panel (exact st count is not crucial to the pattern, as long as it is an even number), turn.

Row 2: Ch 2 (counts as dc), *bpdc in next st, fpdc in next st; rep from * across row.
Fasten off.
Weave in all ends.

Oversized Turtleneck

Designed by Ariel Thongsaly of
The Knitted Sisters

SIZE
XS (S, M, L, XL, 2X, 3X, 4X, 5X)

YARN
Lion Brand Jeans Colors (100%
acrylic; 246 yards [225 m] per
3½ oz [100 g] skein)): 6 (7, 8, 9,
10, 10, 11, 12, 13) skeins #145
Corduroy

HOOK
Size US 7 (4.5 mm) and I/9 (5.5
mm) crochet hooks
Or size needed to obtain gauge

FINISHED MEASUREMENTS

	BUST	WAIST	HIPS
XS	28–30" (71–76 cm)	23–24" (58–61 cm)	33–34" (84–86 cm)
S	32–34" (81–86 cm)	25–26½" (63–67 cm)	35–36" (89–91 cm)
M	36–38" (91–97 cm)	28–30" (71–76 cm)	38–40" (97–101 cm)
L	40–42" (101–107 cm)	32–34" (81–86 cm)	42–44" (107–112 cm)
XL	44–46" (112–117 cm)	36–38" (91–97 cm)	46–48" (112–122 cm)
2X	48–50" (122–127 cm)	40–42" (101–107 cm)	52–53" (132–135 cm)
3X	52–54" (132–137cm)	44–45" (112–114 cm)	54–55" (137–140 cm)
4X	56–58" (142–147 cm)	46–47" (117–119 cm)	56–57" (142–145 cm)
5X	60–62" (152–157 cm)	49–50" (124–127 cm)	61–62" (155–157 cm)

NOTIONS

Stitch markers

GAUGE

17 sts and 16 rows = 4" (10 cm) in ribbing with smaller hook
15 sts and 14 rows = 4" (10 cm) in Lemon Peel st with larger hook

SPECIAL STITCHES

Lemon Peel Stitch (see page 173)

LEMON PEEL INCREASE ROW (ALWAYS WORKED ON ROW 1 OF PATTERN)

Increase row: Ch 2 (does not count as dc), (dc, sc) in first st, dc in next st, *sc in next st, dc in next st; rep from * to last st, (sc, dc) in last st, turn.

NOTES

- You will be working sc into the top of dc sts, and dc into the top of sc sts.
- Sweater is designed to be oversized. If you want it more fitted, go down a size. If you want it even more oversized, go up a size.

SWEATER PATTERN

BODY (MAKE 2)
RIBBING

Using smaller hook, make a slip knot, leaving a long tail for seaming side of sweater.

Row 1: Make sc foundation ch of 16 (16, 18, 18, 20, 20, 22, 22, 22) sts, turn.

Note: For more stability for seaming, sc in the first st of all even rows and in the last st of all odd rows; cont with sc blo for the rest of the row.

Row 2: Ch 1, sc blo across, turn. Rep Row 2 for a total of 75 (79, 87, 93, 101, 111, 115, 119, 127) rows.

Turn work 90 degrees and change to larger hook. Working 1 st in every ribbing row:

Row 1 (WS): Work in Lemon Peel st, turn—75 (79, 87, 93, 101, 111, 115, 119, 127) sts.

Rows 2–28 (28, 30, 30, 32, 32, 34, 34, 34): Cont in Lemon Peel st, turn.

Note: For more length, add as many rows as you would like; just be sure to end on an even row.

Rows 29 (29, 31, 31, 33, 33, 35, 35, 35)–30 (30, 32, 32, 34, 34, 36, 36, 36): Work Lemon Peel inc row, turn—79 (83, 91, 97, 105, 115, 119, 123, 131) sts after final row.

Rows 31 (31, 33, 33, 35, 35, 37, 37, 37)–32 (32, 34, 34, 36, 36, 38, 38, 38): Work in Lemon Peel st, turn.

Rows 33 (33, 35, 35, 37, 37, 39, 39, 39)–34 (34, 36, 36, 38, 38, 40, 40, 40): Work Lemon Peel inc row, turn—83 (87, 95, 101, 109, 119, 123, 127, 135) sts after final row.

Rows 35 (35, 37, 37, 39, 39, 41, 41, 41)–36 (36, 38, 38, 40, 40, 42, 42, 42): Work in Lemon Peel st, turn.

Rows 37 (37, 39, 39, 41, 41, 43, 43, 43)–42 (42, 44, 44, 46, 46, 48, 48, 48): Ch 2, work Lemon Peel inc row, turn—95 (99, 107, 113, 121, 131, 135, 139, 147) sts after final row.

Row 43 (43, 45, 45, 47, 47, 49, 49, 49): Work in Lemon Peel st, turn.

Rows 44 (44, 46, 46, 48, 48, 52, 52, 52)–62 (62, 66, 66, 70, 70, 74, 74, 74): Work in Lemon Peel st, turn. Fasten off, leaving a 12" (30.5 cm) tail.

SLEEVES (MAKE 2)
RIBBING

With smaller hook, make a slip knot, leaving a long tail for seaming sleeves.

Row 1: Make a sc foundation ch of 16 (16, 18, 18, 20, 20, 22, 22, 22) sts, turn.

Row 2: Ch 1, sc blo across, turn. Note: For more stability for seaming, sc in the first st of all even rows and the last st of all odd rows, then cont with sc blo for the rest of the row. Rep Row 2 for a total of 35 (35, 37, 37, 39, 39, 41, 41, 41) rows.

SLEEVE BODY

Turn work 90 degrees and change to larger hook. Working 1 st in every ribbing row:

Row 1 (WS): Work in Lemon Peel st—35 (35, 37, 37, 39, 39, 41, 41, 41) sts.

Rows 2–4: Cont in Lemon Peel st, turn.

Rows 5–6: Work Lemon Peel inc row, turn—39 (39, 41, 41, 43, 43, 45, 45, 45) sts.

Rows 7–8: Work in Lemon Peel st, turn.

Rows 9–10: Work Lemon Peel inc row, turn—43 (43, 45, 45, 47, 47, 49, 49, 49) sts.

Rows 11–12: Work in Lemon Peel st, turn.

Rows 13–14: Work Lemon Peel inc row, turn—47 (47, 49, 49, 51, 51, 53, 53, 53) sts.

Rows 15–16: Work in Lemon Peel st, turn.

Size XS only: Cont in Lemon Peel st until Row 31, ignoring inc listed below.

Rows 17–18: Work Lemon Peel inc row, turn— – (51, 53, 53, 55, 55, 57, 57, 57) sts after Row 18.

Rows 19–20: Work in Lemon Peel st.

Sizes S, M, and L only: Cont in Lemon Peel st until Row 32, ignoring inc listed below.

Rows 21–22: Work Lemon Peel inc row, turn— – (–, –, –, 59, 59, 61, 61, 61) sts after Row 22.

Size XL only: Cont in Lemon Peel st until Row 33, ignoring inc listed below.

Rows 23–24: Work Lemon Peel

inc row, turn— – (–, –, –, –, 63, 65, 65, 65) sts after Row 24.

Size 2XL only: Cont in Lemon Peel st until Row 33, ignoring inc listed below.

Row 25: Work Lemon Peel inc row, turn— – (–, –, –, –, –, 67, 67, 67) sts.

Size 3XL only: Cont in Lemon Peel st until Row 33, ignoring inc listed below.

Row 26: Work Lemon Peel inc row, turn— – (–, –, –, –, –, –, 69, 69) sts.

Size 4XL only: Cont in Lemon Peel st until Row 33, ignoring inc listed below.

Row 27: Work Lemon Peel inc row, turn— – (–, –, –, –, –, –, –, 71) sts.

Size 5XL only: Cont working in Lemon Peel st until Row 33. Fasten off, leaving a 12" (30.5 cm) tail.

TURTLENECK RIBBING

Note: The neckline is worked separate from the Body and seamed after. There are two options for the turtleneck: Option A is a more fitted turtleneck and Option B is a looser-fit turtleneck. You can also choose how tall to make your turtleneck, giving you the option of rolling it down once or twice. Number of sts for each roll-down option is noted as ×1 (×2).

With larger hook, make a slip knot, leaving a 14" (35.5 cm) tail.

Row 1: Make a sc foundation ch of 50 (75) sts, turn.

Note: For more stability for seaming, sc in the first st of all even rows and the last st of all odd rows, then cont with the sc blo for the rest of the row.

Row 2: Ch 1, sc blo across, turn.

Option A: Fitted

Rows 3–67: Ch 1, sc blo across, turn.

Fasten off.

Option B: Loose Fitting

Rows 3–75: Ch 1, sc blo across, turn.

Note: If you would like your neckline even looser, cont adding rows here.

Fasten off.

FINISHING

Block each piece.

SEAM SHOULDERS

Place the two body pieces WS together. Note: The option you chose for your turtleneck will determine how many sts you whip st together on each shoulder.

Starting at the edge of the shoulder and using long tails, whip st each shoulder together toward the center, leaving 33 sts unseamed in the center for the neckline. Secure the ends. Place a st marker on the last 2 sts that you whip st together on each side to mark the neckline.

SEAM TURTLENECK RIBBING

Lay out the body so you can easily see the neckline. The last row worked on your ribbing piece will be the tail that you attach to the neckline. Take the long tail and whip st the ribbing to the neckline from one of the stitch markers across the neckline. Tip: Whip st 1 ribbing row to 1 st from the neckline. Cont working a whip st in every ribbing row on the opposite side of the neckline until you have 1 row of the ribbing left. Fasten off. Using the other long tail at the top of the ribbing piece, whip st down the top to the corner st to seam ribbing closed.

SEAM SLEEVES TO BODY

With RS of body and sleeve facing, align the center of the sleeve with the shoulder seam. Tip: Use st markers to attach pieces and help keep everything even. Using the long tail, whip st across to attach the sleeve to the body. Fasten off. Rep on the other side.

SEAM SLEEVES

Using the long tail from the start of the sleeve ribbing, whip st up the sleeve until you get to the underarm where the sleeves meet the body. Fasten off into the first and last st of the sleeve to avoid a hole. Rep for opposite sleeve.

SEAM BODY

Using the tail from the beginning of the body ribbing, whip st up the side of the body to the underarm. Fasten off into the sleeve seam edge to avoid a hole. Rep on the other side of the body.

Tip: By seaming each piece on the RS, you get an amazing seam on the shoulder and side of the sweater.

Weave in ends.

Garden Party Wrap

Designed by Mary Palmentieri

SIZE
One size fits most adults

FINISHED MEASUREMENTS
14½" (37 cm) × 63" (160 cm)

YARN
Lion Brand Beautiful You (100% acrylic; 326 yards [298 m] per 3½ oz [100 g] skein)): 2 skeins each #184 Spanish Villa (Color A) and #149 Glacier Gray (Color B)
Lion Brand Touch of Merino (90% acrylic, 10% Merino; 257 yards [235 m] per 3½ oz [100 g] skein)): 1 skein #098 Gardenia (Color C)

HOOK
Size US G/6 (4 mm) crochet hook
Or size needed to obtain gauge

GAUGE
20 sts and 7 rows = 4" (10 cm) in chevron st

NOTES
- Wrap is worked as one large rectangular panel in a striped chevron pattern.
- Pattern can easily be lengthened by adding more rows. However, this may affect yardage.
- Fringe is optional.
- Knowledge of basic blocking techniques is recommended when making this pattern.
- The stripe sequence in this pattern is completely random.
- All coral and gray stripes are made of two rows: a puff stitch row followed by a single crochet row.
- All white stripes are crocheted in two of the same row.

SHAWL PATTERN

For all coral and gray stripes, you will work Row 3 followed by Row 4.

With Color A, ch 130.

Row 1: Dc in the 4th ch from hook, [dc2tog over the next 2 ch] twice, *[ch 1, hdc3tog in the next 3 ch] 5 times, ch 1,** [dc2tog over the next 2 ch] 6 times; rep from * ending last repeat at **, [dc2tog over next 2 ch] 3 times—68.

Row 2: Ch 1, turn, sc in first st, sc in each st and in each ch-1 sp.

Row 3: Ch 3, turn, skip first st, dc in next st, [dc2tog over next 2 ch] twice, *[ch 1, hdc3tog in next st] 5 times, ch 1**, [dc2tog over next 2 ch] 6 times; rep from * ending last repeat at **, [dc2tog over next two 2 ch] 3 times. Do not work a st in the ch 3 at the end of the row.

Row 4: Ch 1, turn, sc in first st, sc in each st and ch-1 sp.

For all White stripes you will repeat Row 5 twice.

Row 5: Ch 1, turn, hdc in first st, sl st in next st, *hdc in next st, sl st in next st; rep from * to end of row.

Feel free to work your stripes in any order you wish. Here is the order of the stripes you see worked in the Garden Party Wrap shown in the pictures:

FINISHING

Block your work. Weave in ends. Add fringe if desired.

2 Coral	4 Gray	1 White	4 Gray
2 Gray	1 White	2 Coral	1 White
3 Coral	1 Coral	1 Gray	3 Coral
3 Gray	2 Gray	1 White	2 Gray
1 White	4 Coral	3 Coral	1 White
2 Gray	1 Coral	2 Gray	1 Gray
1 White	1 Gray	1 White	3 Coral
2 Gray	1 White	1 Gray	3 Gray
2 Coral	1 Gray	4 Coral	2 Coral
1 White	2 Coral	2 Gray	
2 Coral	2 Gray	1 White	
1 Gray	3 Coral	3 Gray	
1 White	3 Gray	2 Coral	

Lotus Hat

Designed by Makenzie Alvarez

SIZE
To fit Adult

FINISHED MEASUREMENTS
18" (46 cm) in circumference and 8" (20 cm) tall

YARN
Sew Happy Jane Delightful DK (100% superwash Merino; 231 yards [211 m] per 3½ oz [100 g] hank): 1 hank in Siren Call

NEEDLE
Size US 3 (3.25 mm) 32" (81 cm) circular or longer if using Magic Loop (dpns can be substituted)

NOTIONS
Cable needle (cn)
US size D/3 (3.25 mm) crochet hook for provisional cast-on
Stitch marker

GAUGE
24 sts and 32 rows = 4" (10 cm) in Stockinette stitch after blocking

NOTE
You will be cabling with the first and last stitches in the round, changing the order in which they are worked (these rounds are italicized).

SPECIAL STITCHES
1/1 LT: Sl 1 onto cn, hold cn in front, k1tbl, k1tbl from cn
1/1 LPT: Sl onto cn, hold cn in front, p1, k1tbl from cn
1/1 RC: Sl 1 onto cn, hold cn in back, k1, k1 from cn
1/1 RT: Sl 1 onto cn, hold cn in back, k1tbl, k1tbl from cn
1/1 RPT: Sl 1 onto cn, hold cn in back, k1tbl, p1 from cn
2/1 LPC: Sl 2 onto cn, hold cn in front, p1, k2 from cn

2/1 RPC: Sl 1 onto cn, hold cn in back, k2, p1 from cn

PROVISIONAL CAST-ON
This common cast-on is used when stitches are to be worked later. In this pattern it is recommend in order to create an invisible closure on the crown. *Note: The final step has been modified for this pattern.*
1. With scrap yarn and a crochet hook, chain the number of stitches plus extra. Cut the tail, pull it through the last chain.
2. With knitting needle and working yarn, pick up and knit the stated number of stitches through the "bumps" on the back of the chain, leaving a 10" (25 cm) tail. Begin working pattern.
3. To remove the scrap yarn chain (when hat is complete), first thread tapestry needle with the tail of the working yarn, pull

out the scrap yarn tail from the last crochet chain stitch. Gently and slowly pull on the tail to unravel the crochet stitches. *This pattern only:* Carefully place each released stitch on the tapestry needle and sew it through the stitches, pull to close the top of the hat. Weave in end.

HAT PATTERN

Using Provisional CO, CO 9 sts. Pm and join to work in the rnd.

Rnd 1: Knit.

Rnd 2: *K1, m1; rep from * around—18 sts, 9 st inc.

Rnd 3: Knit.

Rnd 4: *K1, m1, p1, m1, k1; rep from * around—30 sts, 12 st inc.

Rnd 5: *K2 p1, k2; rep from * around.

Rnd 6: *K2, m1p, p1, m1p, k2; rep from * around—42 sts, 12 st inc.

Rnd 7: *K2, p3, k2; rep from * to end.

Rnd 8: *K2, m1p, p3, k2, m1p; rep from * around—54 sts, 12 st inc.

Rnd 9: *K2, p4, k2, p1; rep from * around.

Rnd 10: *K2, m1p, p4, k2, m1p, p1; rep from * around—66 sts, 12 st inc.

Rnd 11: *K2, p5, k2, p2; rep from * around.

Rnd 12: *K2, p5, m1p, k2, p2, m1p; rep from * around—78 sts, 12 st inc.

Rnd 13: *K2, p6, k2, p3; rep from * around.

Rnd 14: *K2, m1p, p6, k2, m1p, p3; rep from * around—90 sts, 12 st inc.

Rnd 15: *K2, p7, k2, p4; rep from * around.

Rnd 16: *K2, p7, m1p, k2, p4, m1p; rep from * around—102 sts, 12 st inc.

Rnd 17: *K2, p8, k2, p5; rep from * around.

Rnd 18: *K2, p8, k2, m1p, p2, kfb, p2, m1p; rep from * around—120 sts, 18 st inc.

Note: Starting with Rnd 19, work from either the chart or from written instructions.

Rnd 19: (K2, p8, k2, p3, k1tbl twice, p3), rep to end.

Rnd 20: (2/1 LPC, p6, 2/1 RPC, p3, 1/1 RT, p3), rep to end.

Rnd 21: (P1, k2, p6, k2, p4, k1tbl twice, p3), rep to end.

Rnd 22: (P1, 2/1 LPC, p4, 2/1 RPC, p3, 1/1 RPT, 1/1 LPT, p2), rep to end.

Rnd 23: (P2, k2, p4, k2, p4, k1tbl, p2, k1tbl, p2), rep to end.

Rnd 24: (P2, 2/1 LPC, p2, 2/1 RPC, p3, 1/1 RPT, p2, 1/1 LPT, p1), rep to end.

Rnd 25: (P3, k2, p2, k2, p4, k1tbl, p4, k1tbl, p1), rep to end.

Rnd 26: (P3, 2/1 LPC, 2/1 RPC, p3, 1/1 RPT, p4, 1/1 LPT), rep to end.

Rnd 27: (P5, k2, p5, k1tbl, p6, k1tbl), rep to end.

Rnd 28: Remove marker, sl 1 st onto cn, hold in back, being careful not to wrap working yarn around sts. Sl 1 st from RN onto LN (this is now the first st in rnd). Sl 1 st from cn onto RN (this is now the last st in rnd), pm. Sl 1, (p4, 1/1 RC, p4, 1/1 RPT, p6, 1/1 LPT) 5 times, p4, 1/1 RC, p4, 1/1 RPT, p7.

Rnd 29: (K1tbl, p10, k1tbl, p8), rep to end.

Rnd 30: (1/1 LT, p8, 1/1 RT, p8), rep to end.

Rnd 31: (K1tbl twice, p8), rep to end.

Rnd 32: Remove marker, sl 1 st onto cn, hold in front, being careful not to wrap working yarn around sts. Sl 1 st from RN onto LN (this is now the first st in rnd). Sl 1 st from cn onto RN (this is now the last st in rnd), pm. Sl 1, (1/1 LPT, p6, 1/1 RPT, 1/1 LPT, p6, 1/1 RPT) 5 times, 1/1 LPT, p6, 1/1 RPT, 1/1 LPT, p6, k1tbl.

Rnd 33: (P2, 1/1 LPT, p4, 1/1 RPT, p2, 1/1 LPT, p4, 1/1 RPT), rep to end.

Rnd 34: P3, k1tbl, (p4, k1tbl), rep to last st, p1.

Rnd 35: P3, 1/1 LPT, p2, 1/1 RPT, (p4, 1/1 LPT, p2, 1/1 RPT), rep to last st, p1.

Rnd 36: P4, k1tbl, p2, k1tbl, (p6, k1tbl, p2, k1tbl), rep to last 2 sts, p2.

Rnd 37: P4, 1/1 LPT, 1/1 RPT, (p6, 1/1 LPT, 1/1 RPT), rep to last 2 sts, p2.

Rnd 38: P5, k1tbl twice, (p8, k1tbl twice), rep to last 3 sts, p3.

Rnd 39: P5, 1/1 RT, (p8, 1/1 RT), rep to last 3 sts, p3.

Rnd 40: P5, (k1tbl twice, p18) 5 times, k1tbl twice, p13.

Rnd 41: P4, (1/1 RPT, 1/1 LPT, p16) 5 times, 1/1 RPT, 1/1 LPT, p12.

Rnd 42: P3, (1/1 RPT, p2, 1/1 LPT, p14) 5 times, 1/1 RTP, 1/1 LPT, p11.

Rnd 43: P2, (1/1 RPT, p4, 1/1 LPT, p12) 5 times, 1/1 RPT, p4, 1/1 LPT, p10.

Rnd 44: P1, (1/1 RPT, p6, 1/1 LPT, p10) 5 times, 1/1 RPT, p6, 1/1 LPT, p9.

Rnd 45: (1/1 RPT, p8, 1/1 LPT, p8) rep to end.

Rnd 46: Remove marker, sl 1 onto cn, hold in front, being careful not to wrap working yarn around sts. Sl 1 st from RN onto LN (this is now the first st in rnd). Sl 1 st from cn onto RN (this is now the last st in rnd), pm. Sl 1, (p10, 1/1 LPT, p6, 1/1 RPT) 5 times, p10, 1/1 LPT, p6, k1tbl.

Rnd 47: (P12, 1/1 LPT, p4, 1/1 RPT) rep to end.

Rnd 48: P13, (1/1 LPT, p2, 1/1 RPT, p14) 5 times, 1/1 LPT, p2, 1/1 RPT, p1.

Rnd 49: P14, (1/1 LPT, 1/1 RPT, p16) 5 times, 1/1 LPT, 1/1 RPT, p2.

Rnd 50: P15, (1/1 LT, p18) 5 times, 1/1 LT, p3.

Rnds 51–55: Purl.

Rnds 56–65: *P1, k1tbl; rep from * to end.

BO in pattern.

FINISHING

CLOSING CROWN

With RS facing, thread tail from CO edge onto tapestry needle. Remove scrap yarn as indicated in Notes; thread live sts carefully onto tapestry needle. Pull yarn to close crown. Thread yarn through center to WS and secure.

Weave in ends.

Block; allow to dry completely.

CABLE CHART

Note: Chart begins on Rnd 19 after all increases have been made.

Repeat section is marked in red box.

Sts in gray boxes cable at the beginning of the rnd where first st and last st in the rnd are cabled.

Cable Chart

Chart Key

☐ knit	● purl	1/1 LT	1/1 RT
Ω k tbl	V slip	1/1 RC	2/1 LPC
℧ m1	1/1 LPT	1/1 RPT	2/1 RPC

ABBREVIATIONS & HOW-TO

ABBREVIATIONS

bl: back loop

Bldc: back loop double crochet

Bpdc: back post double crochet

blo: stitch in the back loop only

Blsc: back loop single crochet

BOR: beginning of round

CC: contrast color

cdc: crossed double crochet: skip next stitch, double crochet in next st, double crochet in skipped stitch

ch: chain

cn: cable needle

CO: cast on

cont: continue

dc: double crochet

dec: decrease

Esc: extended single crochet

Esc2tog: extended single crochet two together (decrease)

Fdc: foundation double crochet

Fpdc: front post double crochet

Fptr: front post treble crochet

Fsc: foundation single crochet

hdc: half double crochet

inc: increase

k2tog: knit two together (right-slanted decrease)

k: knit

k1tbl: knit 1 through the back loop

kfb: knit into front and back of stitch

LN: left needle

m1: make 1 stitch knitwise (increase)

m1p: make 1 stitch purlwise (increase)

MC: main color

p: purl

pm: place marker

rep: repeat

RN: right needle

RS: right side

sc: single crochet

sc2tog: single crochet two together

sc dec: single crochet decrease

sk: skip

sl: slip

sl st: slip stitch

sm: slip marker

sp: space

ssk: slip, slip, knit (left-slanted decrease)

st: stitch

St st: Stockinette stitch

tbl: through the back loop

tl: third loop

WS: wrong side

yo: yarn over

HOW-TO

FRINGE

1. Wrap your yarn around a card, book, or other item that's the length you want your fringe. You'll need 2–3 wraps for each piece of fringe, depending on how thick you want it.
2. Cut across the bottom edge, so you have separate strands all the same length.
3. Separate the strands into groups of 2–3, still folded in half.
4. Insert a crochet hook from back to front between stitches at one end of the edge where you want to add the fringe. Use the hook to pull the folded end of a piece of fringe through from front to back, creating a loop. Then pull the ends of yarn through the loop, and pull to secure—snug but not too tight.
5. Repeat across the edge of your project. Trim the ends to even the fridge, if desired.

LEMON PEEL STITCH

Row 1 (WS): Ch 1, sc in first st, *dc in next st, sc in next st; repeat from * to end of row, turn.
Row 2: Ch 2 (does not count as dc), dc in first st, *sc in next st, dc in next st; rep from * to end of row, turn.

WRAP

Wrap the nonworking yarn around the working yarn counterclockwise as if catching a colorwork float. The wrap is to be worked after the knit stitch that the symbol is on is knit. Snug up the wrap to the base of the last st worked, but do not pull too tightly on the yarn. When you work the stitches before and after the wrap, think of them as a colorwork st: Do not pull so tightly that it bunches your work, but do not leave it loose enough to cause holes or big floats.

W&T (WRAP AND TURN)

Right side (knit stitches): Bring yarn forward, slip next stitch to right needle, bring yarn to back of work, slip stitch back to left needle. Turn work.
Wrong side (purl stitches): Bring yarn to the back, slip next stitch to right needle, bring yarn to front of work, slip stitch back to left needle. Turn work.

WORKING STITCHES WITH WRAPS

Slip wrapped stitch to the right needle. Using the tip of the left needle, pick up the wrap. (Note that if the stitch has two wraps, pick up both wraps.) Place the slipped stitch back onto the left needle, alongside the wrap. For knit stitches, knit the stitch and its wrap together through the back loop. For purl stitches, purl the stitch and its wrap together.

ACKNOWLEDGMENTS

This book would not be complete and would have not been possible without the amazing support from so many people.

First and foremost, to the entire Our Maker Life community: Thank You. OML's continued growth and advancement were founded on the love and belief that the movement was even a possibility, and for that, the entire OML leadership and publishing team will forever be grateful. Through every hurdle and step overcome, your support has been a constant companion on this journey, and we do not, nor will we ever, take that support lightly. Thank you for being as excited and passionate about OML as we are! Thank you for pushing the movement forward—for sharing your designs, dreams, and work with us, so that we may continue to share them with the world. There is no OML without the community, and we are forever humble and appreciative that so many of you continue to follow and take such creative strides with us on social media, at our events, and through the support and sharing of our published work. We dedicate this book to you.

To our leadership, publishing, editing, and marketing teams: Thank You. More than a year of work has been poured into bringing this book to life, and it is profoundly recognized. Your dedication in working as a leadership team and with all of our contributors displays the power of teamwork and how wonderful our industry is when collaborative goals are able to flourish! Thank you for the hours upon hours that you've put in to make this book happen; we are forever proud and grateful. Meredith at Abrams Books, thank you for taking the beginning, middle, and finishing steps with us, particularly through your exuberance and excitement that this book was a possibility, and for believing in us to bring the vision and work to life.

To our contributors: Thank You. This book hands down would not have been possible without your amazing creative art. Every image, word, story, and pattern makes our heart beat in a special way, and we know the world will be that much brighter for our having the honor and opportunity to share it! Thank you for your patience, availability, dedication, hard work, and willingness to believe in the OML leadership and publishing team to ensure that this book was completed and presented in a way that we all can be proud of.

There are so many more people who have made Our Maker Life a possibility and whom we hold immense honor and gratitude toward. We have no doubt that we were able to produce this book because of how large the overall OML movement is, has become, and will continue to be—and so to every person who has made that possible, we thank you and we celebrate you. To every person who experiences a spark of joy from these stories and patterns, and utilizes that to share and do something great in their own maker life, we thank you as well. At its core, our hope for this book is really embedded in that— that it inspires you to make. We have a strong belief that it will, and we're excited about what that will look like, whether it be with the jump start of a new small business, a new pattern release, a cozy photo shoot, or a new knitting website—we know this craft is a revolving door of inspiration, and even if we unlock that potential in just one person, we believe it will be well worth it.

"For makers, by makers" is what we stand for, and we hope that in some small or grand way, this book showcases that stand, rise, and step forward in our community and industry, from first page to last.

Editor: Meredith A. Clark
Designer: Darilyn Lowe Carnes
Production Manager: Rachael Marks

Library of Congress Control Number: 2020944092

ISBN: 978-1-4197-4713-7
eISBN: 978-1-68335-993-7

Printed and bound in China
10 9 8 7 6 5 4 3 2 1

Abrams books are available at special discounts when purchased in quantity
for premiums and promotions as well as fundraising or educational use.
Special editions can also be created to specification. For details, contact
specialsales@abramsbooks.com or the address below.

Abrams® is a registered trademark of Harry N. Abrams, Inc.

ABRAMS The Art of Books
195 Broadway, New York, NY 10007
abramsbooks.com